Headlong and Liverpool Everyman & Playhouse
present the world premiere of

CORRINA, CORRINA

BY CHLOË MOSS

Commissioned by Headlong,
the first performance of *Corrina, Corrina*
was at the Everyman Theatre, Liverpool
on 17 May 2022.

CORRINA, CORRINA

BY CHLOË MOSS

ANGELO	James Bradwell
CAPTAIN	David Crellin
CORRINA	Laura Elsworthy
WILL	Mike Noble
RIZAL	Angelo Paragoso
RAFAEL	Martin Sarreal
Director	Holly Race Roughan
Set and Costume Designer	Moi Tran
Sound Designer and Composer	Max Perryment
Lighting and Video Designer	Joshua Pharo
Movement Director	Chi-San Howard
Dramaturg	Mingyu Lin
Assistant Director	Ericka Posadas
Audio Description	Anne Hornsby
Casting Director	Amy Ball
Production Manager	Sam Paterson
Fight Director	Kate Waters
Costume Supervisor	Jacquie Davies
Stage Manager	Gemma Dunne
Deputy Stage Manager	Olivia Roberts
Assistant Stage Manager	Charlotte Jones
Lighting Programmer and Operator	Jack Coleman
Sound Operator	Keiran Sing
Sound Engineers	Ian Davies Rob Newman
Wardrobe Manager	Shellby Harmer
Set Construction and Paint	RT Scenic
Stage Crew and Automation	Mike Cantley Jack Coleman
Stage Crew	Jack Higham Christian Cheevers
Video Associate	Sarah Readman

James Bradwell | Angelo

James is a British-Filipino actor. He trained at the Bristol Old Vic Theatre School.

Theatre credits include: *My Night with Reg* (Turbine Theatre); *Romeo & Juliet, Richard III* (Shakespeare's Rose Theatre, Oxford); *Welcome to Thebes* (Tobacco Factory) and *Dracula* (Loco Klub).

Television credits include: Recently wrapped as a series regular on *I Hate You* by Robert Popper for Channel 4, *Holby City, The Split* (BBC); *Cbeebies Presents: Romeo & Juliet* (CBeebies); *Murder They Hope* (UKTV); *Back to Life* (Netflix) and *Victoria* (ITV)

Video Game credits include: *Nioh 2, Horizon: Forbidden West* (Sony) and multiple projects with PitStop Productions TBA.

David Crellin | Captain

Theatre credits include: *Kes* (Liverpool Playhouse); *Wuthering Heights, West Side Story, There is a Light, Happy Days, The Mighty Walzers, Saturday Night Sunday Morning* (Royal Exchange Theatre); *The Ockerbys on Ice* (Dukes Theatre); *The Hoard Festival* (New Vic, Newcastle); *The Seagull, Hard Times, Audience, Much Ado About Nothing, Rock N Roll, Beyond Belief, Audience, Schweyk In The Second World War, Measure For Measure* (Library Theatre); *All of You Mine, Spring and Port Wine* (Bolton Octagon); *Absent Friends* (Oldham Coliseum, Harrogate Theatre, Basingstoke Haymarket Theatre); and *Get Ken Barlow* (Watford Palace).

Radio credits include: *A Grain Of Truth, Blood Sex and Money, Entanglement, Craven, Poor Obscure Plain and Little, L'Assommoir, Night On The Town, Because You're Not, It's Your Move* (BBC Radio 4); *The Provoked Wife, The Palimpsest, Watcher In The Rye* (BBC Radio 3) and many other audio dramas and stories.

Television credits include: *Time, Years & Years, Moving On, Doctors, Happy Valley, Home Fires, Holby City, Accused, Shameless, Coronation Street, Paradox, Mysterious Creatures, The Girls Who Came To Stay, What We Did On Our Holidays, North & South, The Bill, Dalziel & Pascoe* and *Blood Strangers.* And series regular in *Emmerdale, Heartbeat, The Cops, Waterloo Road, Fat Friends*.

Film credits include: *Hillsborough, Strumpet, Vacuuming Completely Nude In Paradise* and *Heart*

Laura Elsworthy | Corrina

Theatre credits include: *Romeo & Juliet, The Last Testament Of Lilian Bilocca, The Kitchen Sink, The Flint Street Nativity* and *Spacewang* (Hull Truck Theatre); *The Taming Of The Shrew, As You Like It, Miss Littlewood, Mrs Rich and The Hypocrite* (Royal Shakespeare Company); *The Skriker, The Accrington Pals* (Royal Exchange Theatre, Manchester); *Villette* (West Yorkshire Playhouse); *Our Town* (Almeida Theatre); *Macbeth* (MIF/Park Avenue Armory) and *Cooking With Elvis* (Derby Theatre).

Film credits include: *Testament Of Youth* (BBC/Heyday) and *Cinderella* (Disney).

Television credits include: *Vera* (ITV); *Lillian Bilocca* (BBC); *A Midsummer Nights Dream* (Cbeebies); *Plebs* (Rise Films) and *Doctors* (BBC One).

Angelo Paragoso | Rizal

Born and raised in Manila, Angelo trained with Repertory Philippines, Powerdance Philippines, Philippine Ballet Theater and The Royal Conservatoire of The Hague.

Theatre credits include: *The Reporter* (National Theatre); *Miss Saigon* (UK Tour); *Doctor Atomic* (English National Opera); *The King & I* (Royal Albert Hall); *Paper Dolls* (Tricycle Theatre); *Aladdin* (Theatre Royal Stratford East) and *Pearls of the East* (Pinoy Theatre).

Radio credits include: *Writing The Century: Tiger Wings, The Secret Pilgrim* and *The Honourable Schoolboy* (BBC Radio 4 Drama).

Television credits include: *Haunted* (Netflix).

Film credits include: *Paddington 2* (Marmalade Films Ltd.); *Wonka* (Narrow Mark Films Limited); *Nocebo* (Lovely Productions Ireland); *Raging Grace* (Last Conker) and *As You Know Me* (Earls Court Film Festival).

Martin Sarreal | Rafael

Martin trained at Drama Centre London

Theatre credits include: *Sin* (Royal Court); *Finding José* (Arcola Theatre); *Forty Years On* (Chichester Festival Theatre); *The Duke of Milan* (Read not Dead/Shakespeare's Globe); *Romeo & Juliet* (Papergang Theatre); *The Stone* (Bunker Theatre); *The Emperor and the Nightingale* (Theatre by the Lake) and *Here Lies Love* (National Theatre).

Radio credits include: *U.Me* (BBC World Service).

Television credits include: *East Mode* (Comedy Central UK).

Film credits include: *Luther* (BBC Films/Netflix).

Mike Noble | Will

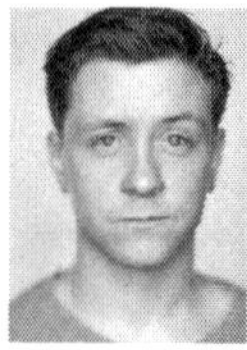

Mike was recently seen in Channel 4's *Help* alongside Jodie Comer and Stephen Graham, as well as Jed Mercurio's new TV series *Trigger Point*. Pre-pandemic he played Matt Haig in the highly anticipated stage adaptation of *Reasons to Stay Alive*.

Theatre credits include: *Love, Love, Love*; *Punk Rock* (Lyric Hammersmith); *Reasons to Stay Alive* (Sheffield Theatres/ETT); *Cougar* (Orange Tree); *The Almighty Sometimes* (Manchester Royal Exchange); *Bad Roads*, *Road* (Royal Court); *Game* (Almeida); *Port*, *The Curious Incident of the Dog in the Night-Time* (National Theatre); *Mudlarks* (Bush Theatre/Hightide).

Film credits include: *Falling into Place*, *Dark River*, *The Siege of Jadotville*, *Bachelor Games*, *Kill Command*, *Jack Ryan: Shadow Recruit*, *World War Z*, *Jadoo*, *Gambit*, *Private Peaceful*.

Television credits include: *Help*, *Trigger Point*, *The Capture*, *Homefires*, *Mr Selfridge*, *Grantchester*, *Prisoners Wives*.

Chloë Moss | Writer

Chloë is an accomplished playwright and screenwriter. Her celebrated play *This Wide Night* (Clean Break/ Soho) won the prestigious Susan Smith Blackburn Prize and was subsequently produced Off-Broadway. Chloë has written numerous other shows including *The Gatekeeper* (Royal Exchange Theatre); *Fatal Light* (Soho); *Christmas is Miles*

Away (Bush/Off-Broadway); *How Love is Spelt* (Bush/New York's Summer Play Festival) and *Run Sister Run* (Pains Plough/Soho Theatre/Sheffield Theatres).

She is currently under commission to the Royal Court and Headlong Theatre.

Chloë has also written extensively for television. She is currently developing original TV projects and is working on an original teen drama for CBBC. She is also under commission to BBC Radio 4.

Holly Race Roughan | Director

Holly Race Roughan is a director of new work and Artistic Director of Headlong.

Theatre credits include: Most recently for Headlong she co-created *Signal Fires*, a nationwide festival for touring companies, and directed *The Ghost Caller* by Luke Barnes, an interactive audio drama for the city of Liverpool. Previously for Headlong she directed the Ibsen adaptation *Hedda Tesman* by Cordelia Lynn, and the UK tour of *People, Places and Things* by Duncan MacMillan. Holly was Co-Director on *Metamorphoses* for Shakespeare's Globe and the Director of the Lyric Ensemble at the Lyric Hammersmith between 2018 and 2019, directing *The Mob Reformers* by Omar El-Khairy. Other directing credits include *Broken Dreams* by Simon Longman for the Royal Court, *Prurience* for Southbank Centre in London and the Guggenheim Museum in New York, *Eye of a Needle* for Southwark Playhouse, Milly Thomas' *A First World Problem* and *Clickbait* for Theatre503, and *Best Served Cold* by Cordelia Lynn for the VAULT Festival. Holly sits on the board of arts-in-prisons charity Kestrel Theatre Company, where she was Associate Director from 2015 to 2019.

TV and Film credits include: She was an Executive Producer on *Unprecedented*, the BBC Four, Century Films and Headlong drama anthology, directing *House Party* by April De Angelis and *Penny* by Charlene James for the series.

Ericka Posadas | Assistant Director

Ericka is an actor and is making her directing debut.

Theatre credits include: *Miss Philippines,* (New Earth Theatre, London); *Gentleman Anne,* (Fabulamundi Playground); *Butterfly*, (VAULT Festival); *West Side Story*, (Royal Exchange Manchester); *Sleeping Beauty* (Theatre Royal Stratford East, London).

Film credits include: *Trip The Light Fantastic* (2022), *The Gallery* (2021), *Silent Disco In The Sky* (2020), *As You Know Me* (2019), *Shift* (2018).

Moi Tran | Set and Costume Designer

Moi is a multi-disciplinary artist, performance maker and set and costume designer. She is founder of East Asian Ticket Club, an engagement platform for the East Asian community.

Theatre credits include: *Rare Earth Mettle, White Pearl* (Royal Court); *Raya, Deluge* (Hampstead Theatre); *The Letters Project* (Gate Theatre); *In the Blood* (Donmar Warehouse); *Chiaroscuro* (Bush Theatre); *Summer Rolls* (Park); *Dear Elizabeth* (Gate Theatre).

Art credits include: *Civic Sound Archive* (PEER); *Sign Chorus* (National Archives); *Shy God A Chorus* (SPILL); *Art Inside Out* (GIBCA); *SHY GOD Chapter Một* (Chisenhale); *I love a broad margin to my life* (Yeo Workshops);*The Bolero Effect* (Hanoi/British Council); *Civic Voice Archive* (The National Archives Fund/UEL).

Dance credits include: *The Circuit* (Prague Quadrennial); *Beats'n'Shine* (MUDAM); *Human Wall* (V&A); *Temporality in a Cut* (Display Gallery).

Opera credits include: *The Imperfect Pearl* (Corn Exchange, Newbury/ St George's, Bristol/King's Place/UK tour); *Falstaff* (Opera Berbiguieres, France).

Film credits include: *Man X* (short); *Bites* (short); *Kolya* (short animation); *Healthy, Join the Dots.*

Awards include: JMK Award for Design.

Joshua Pharo | Lighting and Video Designer

Joshua works as a Lighting and Video Designer across theatre, dance, opera, music, film and art installation.

Theatre credits include: *Kerbs* (Graeae & Belgrade Theatre); *Jekyll & Hyde – Schools Tour* (NT); *Love and Other Acts of Violence* (Donmar Warehouse); *Wolf Witch Giant Fairy* (Royal Opera House); *Extinct* (Theatre Royal Stratford East); *The Litten Trees* (Fuel Theatre); *Crave* (Chichester Festival Theatre); *The Bee in Me* (Unicorn Theatre); *Cinderella* (Lyric Hammersmith); *Vassa* (Almeida); *Noughts & Crosses* (UK Tour); *Going Through* (Bush Theatre); *Future Bodies* (Home Manchester); *Nanjing* (Sam Wanamaker Playhouse) *Medea* (Gate Theatre); *Removal Men* (Yard Theatre); *La Tragédie De Carmen* (Royal Opera House/ Wilton's Music Hall); *Cosmic Scallies* (Royal Exchange/ Graeae); *Burning Doors* (Belarus Free Theatre); *Bodies* (Royal Court); *How My Light Is Spent* (Royal Exchange); *Scarlett* (Hampstead Theatre/ Theatr Clywd); *The Twits* (Curve Theatre); *Contractions* (Crucible Theatre); *Julie* (Northern Stage); *We're Stuck!* (China Plate); *The Bear/The Proposal* (Young Vic).

TV & Film credits include: *Where I Go* (*Where I Can't Be Who I Am*) for Rachel Bagshaw & China Plate.

Max Perryment | Composer and Sound Designer

Max is a Composer and Sound Designer for theatre, TV, dance and commercials.

Theatre credits as Composer include: *Romeo and Juliet* (The Globe); *Shipwreck* (Almeida Theatre).

As Composer and Sound Designer: *Jitney* (Old Vic/Leeds Playhouse); *Miss Julie* (Chester Storyhouse/UK tour); *The Convert* (Young Vic, Main House); *The Sweet Science of Bruising* (Wilton's Music Hall/Southwark Playhouse); *A Guide for the Homesick* (Trafalgar Studio 2); *Utility* (Orange Tree Theatre); *Romeo and Juliet* (Orange Tree Theatre); *Rasheeda Speaking* (Trafalgar Studio 2); *The Tide* (Young Vic, YV Taking Part); *Dear Brutus* (Southwark Playhouse).

As Sound Designer: *Is God Is* (Royal Court Downstairs); *Living Newspaper* (Royal Court); *In A Word* (Young Vic); *Dust* (NYTW, Trafalgar Studio 2, Soho); *The Rise and Fall of Little Voice* (Park Theatre); *Twilight Los Angeles 1992* (The Gate); *Broken Dreams* (Kestral Theatre: HMP Springhill and Royal Court); *Start Swimming* (Young Vic, Summerhall, Edinburgh).

He has written music for feature length documentaries found on Amazon Prime, Apple TV and other platforms such as Vice, and hundreds of TV commercials and brand videos over an 11 year career.

Chi-San Howard | Movement Director

Theatre credits include: *The Taxidermist's Daughter* (Chichester Festival Theatre); *Anna Karenina* (Sheffield Crucible); *Two Billion Beats* (Orange Tree Theatre); *Aladdin* (Lyric Hammersmith); *Milk and Gall* (Theatre503); *Arrival* (Impossible Productions); *Typical Girls* (Clean Break/Sheffield Theatres); *Glee and Me* (Royal Exchange); *Just So* (Watermill Theatre); *Home, I'm Darling*

(Theatre by the Lake/Bolton Octagon/ Stephen Joseph Theatre); *Harm* (Bush Theatre); *Living Newspaper Ed 5* (Royal Court); *Sunnymeade Court* (Defibrillator Theatre); *The Effect* (English Theatre Frankfurt); *The Sugar Syndrome* (Orange Tree Theatre); *Oor Wullie* (Dundee Rep/ National Tour); *Variations* (Dorfman Theatre/NT Connections); *Skellig* (Nottingham Playhouse); *Under the Umbrella* (Belgrade Theatre/ Yellow Earth/Tamasha); *Describe the Night* (Hampstead Theatre); *Fairytale Revolution, In Event of Moone Disaster* (Theatre503); *Cosmic Scallies* (Royal Exchange Manchester/ Graeae); *Moth* (Hope Mill Theatre); *The Curious Case of Benjamin Button*; *Scarlet*; *The Tempest* (Southwark Playhouse); *Adding Machine: A Musical* (Finborough Theatre).

Film credits include: *Hurt by Paradise* (Sulk Youth Films); *Pretending* – Orla Gartland Music Video (Spindle); I *Wonder Why* – Joesef Music Video (Spindle Productions); *Birds of Paradise* (Pemberton Films).

Jacquie Davies | Costume Supervisor

Credits for the Everyman & Playhouse: *Cherry Jezebel, Robin Hood, Our Lady of Blundellsands, Sleeping Beauty, Sweeney Todd, The Snow Queen, Paint Your Wagon, A Clockwork Orange, Othello, The Big I Am, The Little Mermaid, Romeo and Juliet, Conquest of the South Pole, The Story Giant, Fiddler on the Roof, The Sum, Beauty and the Beast, The Odyssey: Missing Presumed Dead, A Midsummer Night's Dream, Little Red Riding Hood, Bright Phoenix, Dead Dog in a Suitcase, Twelfth Night* (Everyman); *The Star, Educating Rita, Juno and the Paycock* and *A View from the Bridge* (Playhouse).

Theatre credits include: *Vurt, Wise Guys, Unsuitable Girls* and *Perfect* (Contact Theatre, Manchester); *Oleanna and Memory* (Clwyd Theatr Cymru); *Love on the Dole* (The Lowry, Manchester); *Never the Sinner* (Library Theatre, Manchester) and *Shockheaded Peter* (West End).

Film & TV credits include: *Queer As Folk, The Parole Officer, I Love the 1970s and 1980s, Brookside* and *Hollyoaks.*

Design credits include: *Kes, Saturday, Sunday, Monday, Oh What a Lovely War, Into the Woods, The Rover, Titus Andronicus, Pericles, Spring Awakening, Twelfth Night, Macbeth, The Red Balloon, The Weirdstone of Brisingamen, Perfect, The Cherry Orchard.*

Amy Ball | Casting Director

Theatre credits include: *Jerusalem* (Apollo Theatre); *Walden, Uncle Vanya* (Harold Pinter); *The Son* (Kiln Theatre/Duke of York's); *The Night of the Iguana* (Noël Coward Theatre); *Sweat* (Donmar Warehouse/Gielgud Theatre); *Rosmersholm* (Duke of York's); *True West* (Vaudeville Theatre); *The Ferryman* (Royal Court/Gielgud Theatre/Bernard B. Jacobs Theatre); *The Moderate Soprano* (Hampstead Theatre/Duke of York's Theatre); *The Birthday Party*, *Who's Afraid of Virginia Woolf?* (Harold Pinter Theatre); *Consent* (National Theatre/Harold Pinter Theatre); *The Goat, or Who Is Sylvia?* (Theatre Royal Haymarket); *Hangmen* (Royal Court/Wyndham's Theatre/Atlantic Theatre Company); *Berberian Sound Studio* (Donmar Warehouse); *The Hunt, Shipwreck, Dance Nation* and *Albion* (Almeida Theatre); *Stories* and *Exit the King* (National Theatre); *A Very Very Very Dark Matter* (Bridge Theatre); *The Brothers Size* (Young Vic) and many further productions for the Royal Court.

At the Everyman & Playhouse, we believe that theatre inspires creative lives. We bring artists, audiences and our communities together in a celebration of what great theatre can achieve.

With two exceptional Liverpool venues united by our mission to entertain and inspire, we create unforgettable experiences built from innovation, talent and a passion for social change.

Whether you visit us at the Everyman or the Playhouse, see our work online or out in the community, we promise you an exhilarating theatrical adventure and a whole new way of looking at the world.

We're grateful for the continued support of Arts Council England, Liverpool City Council, our donors, patrons, partners and our audiences.

Find out more at **www.everymanplayhouse.com**

Chief Executive:
Mark Da Vanzo

Creative Director:
Suba Das

Twitter @LivEveryPlay
Instagram @LivEveryPlay
Facebook @everymanplayhouse

For the Everyman & Playhouse

Leah Abbott Audience Experience Supervisor (Box Office & Stage Door), **Vicky Adlard** Head of Administration, **Robert Awork** YEP Mentor, **Jonty Barlow** Operational Duty Manager Audience Experience, **Eleanor Bartley** Marketing Graphic Design Officer, **Abbie Bates** Audience Experience Manager – Resources, **Francesca Bennett** Marketing Officer, **Ryan Bodell** Audience Experience Supervisor, **Christos Cailleux** Assistant Production Manager, **Michelle Cailleux** Production Coordinator, **Julie Cain** Cleaning Team, **Moira Callaghan** Creativity & Social Change Administrator, **Michael Cantley** Senior Technician – Stage, **Jack Coleman** Senior Technician – Lighting, **Victoria Cuffe** Street Café Manager, **Suba Das** Creative Director, **Ian Davies** Senior Technician - Sound and AV, **Jacquie Davies** Head of Wardrobe, **Lisa Davies** Audience Experience Assistant (Box Office & Stage Door), **Antony Delamere** Facilities Technician, **Stephen Dickson** Finance Manager, **Jake Dooley** Senior Technician – Stage, **Brendan Douglas** Audience Experience Manager (Box Office & Stage Door), **James Duckworth** Operational Duty Manager Audience Experience, **Rachel Elliott-Newton** Venue & Events Planner Commercial, **Ed Freeman** IT Officer, **Natalie Gilmore** Director of Finance and Operations, **Jules Goddard** Audience Experience Assistant (Box Office & Stage Door), **Rosalind Gordon** Relationships Manager, **Ruth Gossage** Head of Commercial Development, **Peter Greggs** Digital Producer, **Helen Grey** Head of Audience Experience, **Helen Griffiths** Audience Experience Manager (Front of House), **Elizabeth Hann** Audience Experience Supervisor, **Joss Harris** Audience Experience Supervisor, **Donald Hart** Cleaning Team, **Rose Hart** Finance Assistant, **Megan Hindley** Audience Experience Supervisor, **Nicola Jackson** Finance Officer, **Melissa James** Audience Experience Supervisor, **Sam Kent** Head of Production, **Andrew King** Marketing Coordinator, **Mike Lancaster** Audience Experience Manager (Food, Bars & Events), **Cathy Lawrence** Audience Experience Assistant (Box Office & Stage Door), **Sarah Lewis** Company Manager, **Gary Lunt** Audience Experience Assistant (Box Office & Stage Door), **Ged Manson** Cleaning Team, **Brod Mason** Temporary Head of Production, **Andrew McKay** Operational Duty Manager Audience Experience, **Louise Merrin** Head of Development, **Eve Mobey** Audience Experience Supervisor, **Nancy Msiska** Stage One Trainee Producer, **Gemma Murrell** Marketing Manager, **Ashlie Nelson** Programmer, **Ian Nenna** Audience Experience Assistant (Box Office & Stage Door), **Robert Newman** Senior Technician – Lighting and AV, **Sarah Ogle** Marketing & Communications Director, **Helen O'Sullivan** Operational Duty Manager Audience Experience, **John Perry** Audience Experience Supervisor, **Francesca Peschier** New Works Associate, **Dominic Phillips** Facilities & Systems Manager, **Ian Redden** Cleaning Team, **Victoria Rope** Senior Producer, **Kath Shaw** HR & Payroll Officer, **Julie Sheridan** Cleaning Supervisor, **Steve Sheridan** Maintenance Manager, **Lewis Shrigley** Audience Experience Supervisor, **Jennifer Tallon-Cahill** Technical Manager, **Christopher Tomlinson** YEP Associate Director, **Leah Wallace** Audience Experience Supervisor (Box Office & Stage Door), **Wesley Warren** Cleaning Team, **Chantal Warren** Cleaning Team, **Mark Da Vanzo** Chief Executive, **Jeffrey Watts** Cleaning Team, **Andy Webster** Senior Technician – Lighting, **Helen Webster** Executive & Artistic Administrator, **Suzie Williams** Operational Duty Manager Audience Experience.

Thanks to all our Audience Experience Team.

Liverpool Everyman & Playhouse are a registered Charity and gratefully acknowledge the support of our funders, donors and audiences.

For their ongoing financial support, we would like to thank:

Garfield Weston Foundation
Backstage
Trust Eleanor Rathbone Charitable Trust
The Johnson Foundation
Creative Access - Mo Siewcharran Fund
Stage One
Noël Coward Foundation
Granada Foundation
Idlewild Trust
Fenton Arts Trust
The Ken Dodd Foundation
P H Holt Foundation

Our HE Partner:
Edge Hill University

Our Business Members & Sponsors:
Benson Signs
Bolland & Lowe
Bruntwood
Duncan Sheard Glass
HA Civils
Hope Street Hotel
Knowsley Chamber of Commerce
Liverpool Growth Platform
Liverpool and Sefton Chamber of Commerce
Make UK
Professional Liverpool
Rathbone Investment Management
Synergy
Wirral Chamber of Commerce
Wrightsure Insurance Group

Our alumni supporters:
Jim Broadbent
Matthew Kelly
Sir Ian McKellen
David Morrissey
Bill Nighy
Eddie Redmayne
Willy Russell
Julie Walters

Our Patrons:
Hilary Banner
John & Mary Belchem
John Birkenhead
Robin Bloxsidge & Nick Riddle
Hilary Fass
Paul Herbert
Brian Higgins
Simon Inch
Richie & Lara Pearn
Anne Pope
Alan Sprince

Those who have left a Legacy or gave an In Memory gift:
Dorothy Smellie Anni Parker & Brian Barry, lovers and supporters of theatre
Malcolm & Roger Frood in memory of Graham & Joan Frood
Michael Key
Fanchon Frolich
The Dunham Family in loving memory of Matthew Dunham, Board Member and friend

Special thanks to those who give monthly or annually for their continued support and to everyone who donated during the pandemic.

Headlong

Headlong is one of the most ambitious and exciting theatre companies in the UK, creating exhilarating contemporary theatre: a provocative mix of innovative new writing, reimagined classics and influential twentieth-century plays that illuminate our world.

Headlong make bold, ground-breaking productions with some of the UK's finest artists. They take these industry-leading, award-winning shows around the country and beyond, in theatres and online, attracting new audiences of all ages and backgrounds.

During an unparalleled period of global uncertainty, Headlong partnered with Century Films and BBC Arts to present *Unprecedented*, a series of critically acclaimed digital plays responding to the radical way that the world changed when the first lockdown was announced.

Previous Headlong productions include *Best of Enemies*, *Hedda Tesman*, *After Life*, *People Places and Things*, *Junkyard*, *The Nether*, *Pygmalion*, *This House*, *Richard III* and *Labour of Love*.

For more information, visit **www.headlong.co.uk**

Twitter @HeadlongTheatre
Instagram @HeadlongTheatre

PR	Kate Hassell & Amy Deering for Bread and Butter PR
Development Manager	Joshua Chua
Marketing Consultant	Stacy Coyne-Wright
Creative Associate	Guy Jones
Writer in Residence	Charlie Josephine
Finance Manager	Keerthi Kollimada
Creative Associate	Mingyu Lin

Executive Director	Lisa Maguire
Assistant Producer	Radha Mamidipudi
General Manager	Rosie Mortimer
Development Consultant	Kirsten Peltonen
Artistic Director	Holly Race Roughan
Producer	Zoë Anjuli Robinson
Community Associate	Iskandar إسكندر R. Sharazuddin
Administration Assistant	Robert Thorpe-Woods

BackstageTrust

COCKAYNE

John Ellerman
Foundation

We are grateful for the generous support of the following Trusts and Foundations:

Backstage Trust
The John Ellerman Foundation
Cockayne – Grants for the Arts
The London Community Foundation

Headlong would like to thank the following individuals for their generous support:

Justin Audibert
Neil and Sarah Brener
Cas Donald
Philip Donald
Annabel Duncan-Smith and Victoria Leggett
Alyce Faye Eichelberger-Cleese
Sarah Ellis
Julia Head
Nick Hern
Richard Huntrods
Jackie Hurt
Nicky Jones
Jack and Linda Keenan
Lil Lambley
Kate Mallinckrodt
Beth and Ian Mill QC
Donna Munday
Rob O'Rahilly
Trevor Phillips
Lesley Wan
Maggie Whitlum

Special thanks

Kanlungan
Father Herbert
Susan Cueva
Choir With No Name
International Seafarers Welfare and Assistance Network
Rose George
Jun Pablo
Felixstowe & Havenport Seafarers Centre
Liverpool John Moores University Maritime Centre
Mandy Redvers Rowe
Leicester Curve
Roel Mayuga
Garizaldy Madarang
Momoko Kitada
Joe Furness

CORRINA, CORRINA

Chloë Moss

For Patricia, my brilliant and beautiful mum

Acknowledgements

Chloë Moss

So many people have helped me during the writing of this play some of whom have spoken to me in confidence about their experiences and are therefore not named below, but I thank them with all my heart.

With huge love and thanks to: Holly Race Roughan and all at Headlong, Mel Kenyon, Frank Peschier, Suba Das, Victoria Rope and all at the Everyman & Playhouse, Moi Tran, Ericka Posadas, Mingyu Lin, Max Perryment, Josh Pharo, Chi-San Howard, Anne Hornsby, Mandy Redvers Rowe, Olivia Roberts, Charlotte Jones, Gemma Dunne, Laura Elsworthy, Mike Noble, James Bradwell, Angelo Paragoso, Martin Sarreal, David Crellin.

Special thanks also to: Jeremy Herrin, Amy Hodge, Alecia Marshall, Amaka Okafor, James Cooney, Jon Chew and Anthony Calf, Nicole Behan, Nina Steiger and all at the National Theatre Studio. Jo Stanley, Rose George, Deborah McPherson, Barbara Kelly, Jessica Tyson, Horatio Clare, Nautilus International, Susan Cueva and Kanlungan, Jun Pablo, Roel Mayuga, Garizaldy Madarang, Momoko Kitada.

And to Franklin Moss Price and Martha Moss Price with all my love.

Characters

CORRINA, *twenty-eight*
THE CAPTAIN, *sixty*
WILL, *thirty*
ANGELO, *thirties*
RAFAEL, *twenty-three*
RIZAL, *forties*

A Note on the Text

A forward slash (/) indicates that the speaker is being interrupted.

This text went to press before the end of rehearsals and so may differ slightly from the play as performed.

ACT ONE

One

May 1st 2022. The port of Felixstowe. The cargo ship MSC Keto in dock. A huge hulking frame, four decks high. Giant container boxes in different bright colours are stacked in rows on top of each other.

The bridge – a horseshoe shaped bank of navigation control equipment in front of a wall of curved panelled windows facing out to sea.

Two black leather chairs sit in front of the navigation station, the helm separating them.

CORRINA *stands in front of the* CAPTAIN.

CAPTAIN. Let me give you a situation. True story. (*Beat.*) About fifteen years ago I was working on an emergency response vessel. Some of the crew were complaining because their cabins were right above the anchor locker and it banged. All night long. Couldn't get any sleep. Chinese bloody torture… Can you still say that? Anyway. The next morning they decide to fix it themselves. Only a small thing… the anchor's loose, needs securing. Simple. Two of them, Victor and Markus, go down to the locker. Victor can't fit inside because he's wearing his protective clothing so he takes it off and climbs in but it's dark… they can't see what they're doing. Markus goes off to get torches. By the time he gets back Victor is *dead*. Chamber rusted; all the oxygen sucked from the air. Last thing he said was heard over the radio 'I'm going to need to put a clip on the anchor' then… Gone. Suffocated in the time it took to say those few words.

Silence.

Third mate equals safety officer. Big responsibility.

Competent mariners make safer ships. Can't afford to make mistakes.

CORRINA. No, Sir.

CAPTAIN. Excellent references from Warsash.

CORRINA. Thank you, Sir.

Silence.

CAPTAIN. What are you doing here?

CORRINA. …

CAPTAIN. What *excites* you about being at sea?

CORRINA. I suppose /

CAPTAIN. 'I love to sail forbidden seas and land on barbarous coasts.' (*Beat.*) *Moby Dick*. That's why *I'm* here… Can you beat that?

CORRINA. My dad was at sea.

CAPTAIN. It's in the blood then. Following in his footsteps.

CORRINA. I suppose so, Sir.

CAPTAIN. Top of your year. Impressive results. (*Beat.*) You were part of an IMO scheme to get more women to sea?

CORRINA. Yes, Sir.

CAPTAIN. Positive discrimination. I'm all in favour. More females on ships. Can only be a good thing. (*Beat.*) Course, you know what they say?

CORRINA. …

CAPTAIN. Bad luck to have a woman on board!

CORRINA. I've heard that one.

CAPTAIN. Bloody nonsense (*Beat.*) See. I might look like a dinosaur but inside I'm a… *progressive*. I like progress. (*Beat.*) Things change. They move on and you have to move on too. Some work the crew too hard, it might be a tight ship but it's not a happy ship.

Silence.

CAPTAIN. What's the plan then? (*Beat.*) After my job?

Beat.

CORRINA. I think I might be, Sir.

CAPTAIN. You *think* you *might?*

CORRINA. Yeah. Yes I want to be Captain, Captain. (*Beat.*) One day.

The CAPTAIN *nods.*

CAPTAIN. Glad to hear it.

CORRINA. Thank you, Sir.

CAPTAIN. Good luck. Any questions… any problems. My door is always open.

CORRINA. Thank you, Sir.

Beat. CORRINA *turns to leave.*

CAPTAIN. Compass deviation.

CORRINA *stops and turns back.*

How do we apply variation and deviation and in what order?

CORRINA. True course in degrees. Apply variation to give us magnetic course. Apply deviation to give us a compass course.

CAPTAIN. TVMDC. (*Beat.*) What's the mnemonic?

CORRINA. True Virgins Make Dull Company.

Beat.

CAPTAIN. True. Virgins. Make. Dull. Company. (*Beat.*) Exactly.

Two

Upper deck. CORRINA *dressed in boiler suit with a clipboard. Some* FILIPINO CREW MEMBERS *are working.*

CORRINA *gestures, a small wave.*

CORRINA. Hi.

A couple awkwardly raise a hand to greet her.

CORRINA. Y'alright?

Silence.

CORRINA. Yeah, I'm a woman. (*Beat.*) Let that sink in for a bit first shall I?

Silence. One of the crew, ANGELO, *pulls an earphone from his ear.*

ANGELO. Their English is not so good. They won't understand.

RAFAEL (*to* ANGELO). Fuck you. My English is perfect.

ANGELO. Last time I sailed with a woman was three… maybe four years ago. She was the cook. Two options for dinner, burnt or cremation. You're in luck this time, Christian is like your guy Gordon Ramsay.

ANGELO *kisses his fingers.*

RAFAEL. You can tell you haven't eaten in a real restaurant for years.

ANGELO *gestures to* RAFAEL *and* RIZAL.

ANGELO. Rafael. And this is Rizal.

They both a mutter reluctant hello to CORRINA.

ANGELO *holds his hand out.*

I'm Angelo. What's your name?

CORRINA. Corrina.

ANGELO. *Corrina.* Like Bob Dylan?

CORRINA. Like Ray Peterson.

ANGELO. Ray Peterson?

CORRINA. American. Nineteen-fifties, you probably won't /

ANGELO *claps his hands together, epiphany.*

ANGELO (*enthusiastically sings the chorus of Ray Peterson's 'Tell Laura I Love Her'*) …then the guy crashes his car and dies. *Man* it's sad!

CORRINA. Same singer, different song.

ANGELO. No sure, sure. Not that song. That's about *Laura.* You're *Corrina.* Hey Corrina! He sings about you too, no?

CORRINA. Not me personally.

ANGELO. Your mother loved this guy, no? Ray Peterson.

CORRINA. My father loved him.

ANGELO. Tell him he's got good taste.

CORRINA. He's dead.

ANGELO. Oh man. I'm sorry.

CORRINA. No need to apologise. Unless you killed him?

ANGELO. Ah come *on.* You can't make jokes about your dead father.

CORRINA. I can make jokes about whatever I fuckin' well like, Angelo. S'called freedom of speech.

RIZAL. Always bad luck for a woman to be on board. (*Beat.*) No offence.

CORRINA. Some taken, I'm not gonna lie.

ANGELO. You get used to it. (*Beat.*) Women. Whistling. Birds.

CORRINA. Thought birds were lucky?

RIZAL. No. *Harming* birds. I sailed years ago with a Turkish Bo'sun. Found a bird on the deck, shitting everywhere. Bird was sick. So he killed it. Snapped its neck, threw it over the side. Out of its misery. Next day Bo'sun lost his whole arm in an accident. (*Gestures.*) Here to here. Ripped off at the shoulder in the engine room. *Same* arm he threw that sick bird with.

CORRINA. So what?

RIZAL. So *punishment*.

RAFAEL. Bullshit.

RIZAL. If he was Russian, Romanian or Bulgarian I don't believe him, but Turkish don't lie.

RAFAEL. Gago!

ANGELO. Look, she thinks we're mad.

CORRINA *shrugs*.

You don't have your own superstitions?

CORRINA. I try and avoid walking under ladders, salute the odd magpie… might throw Scylla a bit of bread.

ANGELO. Scylla?

CORRINA. Sea-monster. Me dad used to tell us about her when I was a kid. She eats sailors. Swims up, thumps on the boat then drags them overboard… so whenever you set foot on a ship you have to chuck her some food and then she might leave you alone.

ANGELO. That's crazy, man. There's no such thing as lady sea-monsters.

CORRINA. But if I whistle we'll all definitely drown?

ANGELO. Hey, I don't really believe in that stuff but you know sometimes I think, why take the risk? So many of them… Open a window in the morning for good luck… cut your nails at night for bad luck… big ears mean long life.

RAFAEL. Then Rizal is immortal.

RIZAL (*ignoring him*). Never walk barefoot on steel.

ANGELO. Don't turn your back on the sea, that's another but it's not very practical on a ship, so I forget about it.

CORRINA. It's all a load of bollocks really isn't it?

ANGELO (*pointing upwards*). You can't say that.

CORRINA. Why not?

ANGELO. You're tempting fate.

CORRINA *looks around. She starts to whistle.*

CORRINA. There you go. (*Beat.*) We're fucked now aren't we?

ANGELO. Yeeeah. You got good jokes. That's funny, man. (*Takes a strip of gum from his pocket and offers it to* CORRINA.) Want some gum?

CORRINA. No thanks. Got my formalisation.

ANGELO. Sure. You wanna make a good impression. Nobody gives a shit about my impression. I chew so much gum I can plug the ship if there's a leak. (*Beat.*) I concentrate good when I chew. It helps your brain, I read a thing somewhere. Stimulates your brain… what do they call them… *Neurons*.

RAFAEL. Why d'you have to talk so much, man?

ANGELO. Last ship I was on. Nobody spoke. Literally nobody. Makes me crazy. I like to talk. People need to talk. No man is an island, hey?

RAFAEL (*to* CORRINA). How many ships you been on?

CORRINA. Enough.

RAFAEL. You look young.

RIZAL. Says Migo Adecer.

ANGELO *laughs.* RAFAEL *scowls.*

ANGELO. This is a boy who won *Starstruck* in the Philippines.

Like you have in the UK… *The X Factor.* He's very good, very talented. *Very young*. My daughter loves him.

RAFAEL *stands and turns on the stereo, a loud fast song.* ANGELO *starts to floss.*

She taught me this. Over Skype. I'm asking about school and what she's learning but she just wants to listen to music. She tells me she's learned to floss, I'm thinking y'know… like… tooth floss. I say, 'Yeah! It's important to floss!' But then she says 'Tatay, I'll show you, I can give you lessons' so I go along with it because y'know, it's *something*. Man, I love it now. I do it in my cabin.

RIZAL. He does it in our cabin.

ANGELO. I'm getting real fast.

RIZAL. Every day.

ANGELO *lets out a whoop and goes faster, swinging his arms and hips as swiftly as possible. He whoops loudly.* RIZAL *stands and switches it off.*

ANGELO. Great exercise in small space.

RAFAEL. You look mentally ill.

ANGELO. Who cares? (*Beat.*) What's that phrase they say? Dance like nobody is watching.

RAFAEL. Nobody *says* that. It's just some shit on posters in those tourist shops.

ANGELO. It's a good phrase. *Positive*. Positivity, man. Come on. I live, I laugh, I love.

RAFAEL. Spending all your money on shit for your children.

ANGELO. What's the problem?

RIZAL. The problem is you don't have tourist money.

ANGELO. It's for my kids, come on! Pasalubong. I never go home empty handed.

RAFAEL. You never go home full stop.

ANGELO *ignores this. He pulls a photo from his top pocket and holds it out to show* CORRINA.

ANGELO. I keep them there. Next to my heart.

CORRINA (*looking at the photo*). Cute.

ANGELO. Aren't they? Super cute. Six and four now. Drive me crazy but man they're funny. Little one is so cheeky. (*Beat.*) I buy them things, what's the problem?

RIZAL. The problem is boxes and boxes in our cabin. You can get rid of it. Put it somewhere else.

ANGELO. C'mon man.

RAFAEL. Rizal doesn't have nobody to buy things for. That's why he's so sensitive. Nobody to waste his money on.

RIZAL. *Waste*. Yes.

ANGELO. Nothing spent on my kids is waste. Not if it makes them smile.

RAFAEL. Few months ago we dock in Singapore. Twelve hour turnaround and Angelo is desperate to go buy his kid some toy she wants /

ANGELO. Nella the Princess Knight. She is a justice-fighting princess with a rotating head.

CORRINA. Like The Exorcist?

ANGELO. She says these ten different phrases and sings Nella the Princess Knight theme tune when you press her courageous heart. (*Beat.*) The small one watches her on the TV every single day.

RAFAEL. He goes, nearly doesn't make it back… risks everything to get this *doll*. Arrives with no time to spare… Guess what we just loaded on board? (*Beat.*) Twenty thousand plastic princesses.

ANGELO. Princess *Knights*. She has a tiara and *armour*. (*Beat.*) Usually we have no clue what's in those things but I'm running back all out of breath with Nella under my arm and I see my friend the stevedore and he shouts 'Hey Angelo! We just loaded a whole container of those.' Maybe he's making fun, I don't know, but it makes me *laugh*.

RIZAL. Boxes and boxes of *things* /

RAFAEL. Useless shit.

ANGELO. Could be *shit* to save your life, man. The world would come to a standstill if it wasn't for us.

RIZAL. I think the world would carry on just fine.

RAFAEL. My cousin spent six months on a Bolivian ship, Inspectors board in Crete, find five thousand shotguns hidden under piles and piles of gymnastic mats.

ANGELO. See? People need gymnastic mats.

RAFAEL. They were for Libyan extremists.

ANGELO. Even terrorists need to exercise.

RAFAEL. Hay naku, the guns, tanga.

RIZAL. Everything is a joke to him. Buys things he doesn't need with the money he gets from shipping the things nobody else needs all across the world.

ANGELO. It's called *life*, my friend. Modern *life*. Life is *good*. You don't need things, Rizal? What about your books?

RIZAL. Books are different. Books are for your mind.

ANGELO (*to* CORRINA, *with a wink*). Thinks he's above everyone else.

RIZAL *shakes his head, refusing to rise to it*.

RAFAEL. Best friends with the Captain.

RIZAL. Hoy, manahimik ka! [Hey, shut up!]

RAFAEL. Goes to visit him in his office. Hey, next time ask for a new basketball hoop for us?

ANGELO. And for him to sort out my wages.

RIZAL. I don't do favours. I don't ask for favours.

ANGELO. C'mon. Y'know what else they say /

RAFAEL. Sino? Sinong 'they'? [Who? Who's 'they'?]

ANGELO. If you are a friend of the captain you can wipe your hands on the sail.

RIZAL. I'm not a friend of the captain.

ANGELO. But you're a friend of me?

RIZAL. No I'm not. Huwag ka nang makialam! [Don't meddle in my business!]

RAFAEL. What *do* you do in there with him Rizal? In fact don't tell me, I don't want nightmares.

RIZAL *picks something up and throws it at* RAFAEL *who is delighted to get a rise out of him.*

RIZAL. Ang lakas mong mang-inis ha? Sige ka… [You really know how to irritate somebody, don't you? Watch it.]

RAFAEL. But at least I don't break the rules (*Beat, pointedly to* CORRINA.) Crew and officers don't mix. For good reason.

CORRINA. And what reason's that?

RAFAEL. Because we get fucked over before long. (*Beat.*) But hey maybe Rizal *wants* to get fucked by the Captain?

RIZAL *is up on his feet he moves towards* RAFAEL *although it's not very convincing as a threat.* RAFAEL *shrieks with laughter.* CORRINA *steps away while* ANGELO *stands in between them.*

ANGELO. Come on man, ignore him!

RIZAL. Tangina mo! Bumalik ka nga dito! [You idiot! Come back here!]

(*Beat, he mutters.*) Gunggong ang puta… [Ignorant bastard…]

RIZAL *retreats and returns to his work.*

ANGELO turns the music back on.

ANGELO. Hey, Rizal. I'll teach you to floss. It's all in the hips. Tara, sayaw tayo!

RIZAL *ignores him.* ANGELO *turns to* CORRINA.

Come on! It's good exercise. (*Beat.*) Like the Libyan gymnastic terrorists. You make your own entertainment hey?

ANGELO *turns the radio back on. He starts to floss.* CORRINA *joins in laughing.*

ANGELO *spots a* SENIOR OFFICER. *He stops abruptly and switches the music off, returning to the rest of the crew who put their heads down and continue working.*

Three

Upper deck. CORRINA *stands alone.* CREW *still working in the background.*

Behind her appears WILL, *uniform, holding a clipboard. He stops, lays the clipboard down and approaches her quietly then picks her up. She screams and spins around. Shock as she registers who it is then she bursts out laughing.*

CORRINA. Fucking… No!

WILL. Saw your name on the list, couldn't believe it.

CORRINA. I had no idea.

WILL. Dodged it would you? Put in for a transfer?

CORRINA. Wouldn't have seen me for dust.

WILL. Thought you dropped off the edge of the earth, mate.

CORRINA. That's impossible apparently. They reckon it's round now.

WILL. Haven't lost it, have yer?

CORRINA. Thought I was shot of you.

WILL. No such luck. (*Beat.*) Won't be weird will it?

Beat.

CORRINA. Why would it be weird?

WILL. Y'know. Your *superior.*

CORRINA. Job title only.

WILL. Course.

CORRINA. Am I still allowed to call you a wanker?

WILL. Disappointed if you didn't.

CORRINA. What about wedgies?

WILL. Only in private. (*Beat.*) Consummate professional now aren't I?

CORRINA. *Consummate.*

WILL. Changed man. Should see me cabin.

CORRINA. Hospital corners is it?

WILL. Bounce a coin off the bed. Eat off the floor.

CORRINA. Good for you.

WILL. Made up to see you, mate.

CORRINA. Me too.

WILL *steps towards* CORRINA. *They hug each other.*

WILL. You look well.

CORRINA. Thanks.

WILL. Been too long. Seen any people recently?

CORRINA. Loads. Step out the house and they're everywhere. It's like they're breeding.

WILL. From college, you arsehole. There was a reunion.

CORRINA. I know.

WILL. It was a laugh. Should've come.

CORRINA. Was I missed then?

WILL. Not really.

CORRINA *gives him the middle finger.*

WILL. Someone said you'd bailed. Working in a bank or something.

CORRINA. A bank?

WILL. Something like that.

CORRINA. Who said that?

WILL. Can't remember.

CORRINA. Fucking *bank*? Are you serious?

WILL. Mightn't have been a bank. Might've been… insurance maybe. *Marketing*.

CORRINA. Oh fuck off.

WILL. Does it matter?

CORRINA. Yeah. It does matter. (*Beat.*) Fucking *bank*.

WILL. Julie's doing shore excursions for a cruise company

CORRINA. Bully for Julie.

WILL. I got it chapter and verse. Homesick, seasick, every kind of sick going. Jumped ship in Singapore, flew straight home.

CORRINA. And you thought I couldn't hack it either?

WILL. *I* never said it.

CORRINA. Believed it though.

WILL (*shrugs*). Hadn't heard about you for a while.

CORRINA. Fuckin' *bank*.

WILL. It's not like they said you joined ISIS (*Beat.*) Julie said she hadn't heard from you neither.

CORRINA. Yeah well, I don't keep in touch with Julie anymore. (*Beat.*) I find her fuckin' draining. She's a drain.

WILL. She is pretty intense.

CORRINA. Suits her working for a… what is it?

WILL. Shore excursions.

CORRINA *laughs.*

WILL. Thought you were bosom buddies.

CORRINA. 'Cause we were the only girls?

WILL. 'Cause it looked like you got on. Heads together all the time, deep in conversation.

CORRINA. We didn't have conversations. Julie talked at me and I sat there. Probably didn't do it to you but she sucked the fuckin' life out of me. (*Beat.*) Remember that day we all got stoned and watched that film where the girl got trapped in a bunker with an alien that made that high pitched screaming noise until she started to bleed out of her eyes? (*Beat.*) That's how Julie made me feel.

WILL. Wow. Sorry I asked. (*Beat.*) Where were you then?

Beat.

CORRINA. How d'you mean?

WILL. Did you bail for a bit? Should be higher up the ranks now, mate. You were the best in the class.

CORRINA. Took some time out.

WILL. How come?

CORRINA. Wasn't sure it was what I wanted to do anymore.

WILL. But now you are?

CORRINA. Yeah.

WILL. I'm glad to hear it, mate.

Silence.

WILL. Impressed the Skipper.

CORRINA. Yeah?

WILL. Said you were 'one to watch'. Put him straight obviously, told him you're a fuckin'… liability.

CORRINA. Best to be honest.

WILL. He give you the happy ship chat? 'Some work the crew too hard. They might run a tight ship.'

CORRINA. 'But it's not a happy ship.'

WILL. He's alright y'know? (*Beat.*) You'll do well on here.

CORRINA. Hope so.

WILL. You will. (*Beat.*) Ready for the off, tomorrow? Too late to back out then.

CORRINA. Who's backing out?

Beat.

WILL. Cargo watch checklist?

CORRINA.…

WILL. The *ten commandments*. What are they?

CORRINA. Now?

WILL. Yeah.

CORRINA. Monitor loading and discharging of cargo. Knowledge of IMDG containers loaded onboard. (*Beat.*) Check lashings and ballast. Inspection of ship's draught. (*Beat.*) Carry out change of watch procedure. Ensure utmost level of safety and security. (*Beat.*) Lashings of out of gauge cargo. Carry out cargo completion without errors.

WILL. Nailed it.

CORRINA. Obviously.

Beat.

WILL. Anything you need. I'm here for you. (*Beat.*) Genuine offer, less of the side-eye.

CORRINA. Thanks.

WILL. Show you the ropes then, shall I?

The sound of the ships bell then a long low horn sound as the ship sets sail.

Four

CORRINA *and* ANGELO *working.* RAFAEL *is in the background with his headphones on.*

CORRINA. You ever seen a blue whale, Angelo?

ANGELO. Twice. In ten years. (*Beat.*) First time there was one with her calf. I was getting worried because she's so near to the ship. Lots of blue whales die like this, nobody can even tell it happens so half of me is like… fuck wow man this is incredible, other half is like… No get away… go on, move away from the ship!

CORRINA. My dad told me he swam next to a blue whale once. Didn't believe him but I thought I might get to see one.

ANGELO. That would be my dream. To swim with one. Maybe he was telling the truth?

CORRINA. Maybe. (Beat.) When I was a kid me mum'd take us to the beach. She'd point out boats in the distance and I'd leg it to the edge of the water and jump up and down shouting like mad, 'Dad! Daddy, dad!' Then I'd worry that Scylla would hear and she'd drag him down to the bottom of the sea.

ANGELO. I can see you as a little girl. Bet you got pigtails.

CORRINA. Never had pigtails. Not a girlie girl. (*Beat.*) Pink dresses, ponies. All that shit.

ANGELO. You a lesbian?

CORRINA. Fuckin' business is it is of yours?

ANGELO. I don't care if you're lesbian. My cousin is lesbian. She's a good woman. (*Beat.*) You could be lesbian, you could be whatever you like. Live and let live, that's what I believe. All this hatred in the world. Crazy, no?

They carry on working. ANGELO *singing quietly.*

CORRINA. You've got a good voice.

ANGELO. I *have* got good voice. Part practise, part gift from God.

CORRINA. Very modest n'all .

ANGELO. We sing, you should join us (*Beat.*) Karaoke.

CORRINA. Oh I don't sing.

ANGELO. Doesn't matter.

CORRINA. I'm no expert but I'd say it's a pretty fundamental part of karaoke.

ANGELO. Karaoke is all about your heart. Not your voice.

CORRINA. Yeah well, my heart doesn't like singing either.

ANGELO. That's sad.

CORRINA. Tragic.

ANGELO. I sing for my family. Keeps me sane. At sea for nearly a year sometimes. Would you believe it if I told you I'm actually an incredibly shy person?

CORRINA. No, Angelo. I wouldn't.

ANGELO. Exactly. It's all inside. Singing helps. It's therapeutic. Helps you relax. Helps you sleep. Very good stress reliever. In every Filipino's contract it's right there. *Karaoke*.

CORRINA. Karaoke's in your *contract*?

ANGELO. About the only thing they do for us. The big bosses *love* it. They love *us*. Speak good English, hardworking, cheap cheap cheap… least they can do is buy a small machine, two hundred pound maximum. (*Beat.*) I knew a guy. He was from Daraga, I'm also from Daraga. Small town. Rural. If you dream to be a rice farmer it's fantastic. I sail with him a lot and each time I notice him slipping. You know? *Slipping*. He's holding on but I can see it behind his eyes. Smile only with his mouth. He's just actions. Like a robot.

We don't know this at the time. But one night he's decided in his head. It's enough for him yeah? He's checking out. We finish our shift and we go down to our room and we write down our songs and we wait our turn. And everyone's usually so impatient because we want to sing our song you know? But. My friend says he can't think what to sing.

Then I know. Something is wrong with this man.

But I don't say it because he's private, a very private person. I just think I'm gonna keep my eyes on him tonight. I'm gonna watch him. Then I sing my song and I look up and he's gone. So I go out to find him and I can feel like something bad is happening then I see him. Up on the rails. He's gonna jump, yes? So my heart is like, oh my God man… *pounding*. I'm creeping towards him trying to be calm. I hold out my hand and I say, 'Come on my friend.' He waits for a while then he gets down.

We walk back in silence then he heads over to the microphone and he sings 'Jolene' by Dolly Parton. I'm watching and smiling but my hands are shaking so bad the whole time, I have to do this behind my back. (ANGELO *gestures.*) Afterwards he says he was just getting some air. But I know. Two years later he has a baby girl, guess what he calls her?

CORRINA. Jolene.

ANGELO. *Dolly,* man! Because Dolly Parton saved his life, yeah? (*Beat.*) That was six years ago. I haven't seen him since. We're always on different boats.

CORRINA. Ships that pass in the night.

ANGELO. You *never* sing?

CORRINA. No. When me dad came home we used to sing together. Celine Dion, mostly.

ANGELO. Celine Dion is an *angel*. Hey, we could do the song from Titanic the movie together. You know it? You got nice eyes like her. I'm not being sleazy. I'm a married guy, remember. I love my wife.

ANGELO *takes a photo from his pocket sticks a photo under* CORRINA*'s nose*.

This was a perfect day. The best day. (*Beat*.) She works in Malaysia now. Fancy hotel resort. Some rich people out there. She gets nice tips.

CORRINA. What about your kids?

ANGELO. They live with their grandparents in the Philippines. We both make it home one year ago. But this is all for them. We save and they do something with their lives. Dollar for homesick. You got kids? Husband?

CORRINA. No.

ANGELO. Single life is better at sea. Less pain, man.

CORRINA. Reckon single life's better anywhere, Angelo.

ANGELO. But lonely?

CORRINA. You must be lonely? Away from your family?

ANGELO. No. I got them here.

ANGELO *taps his pocket*.

ANGELO. I miss them, sure. But it's not the same, not like real loneliness. (*Beat*.) I tell them we're connected always. (*Beat*. *He gestures*.) We're like this… tied together. Invisible rope. Strong connection. Even after life. (*Beat*.) It's like your father. When did he pass?

CORRINA. Long time ago.

ANGELO. That is why you must carry photographs. Look at them all the time. Then you never forget.

CORRINA. Don't need a photo to remember him.

ANGELO. Still. (*Beat.*) It's nice, hey? You keep him with you. And he's with you, right? Watching all the time. (*Beat.*) You make him proud.

CORRINA. I don't really believe in any of that.

ANGELO. No no no. He is with you.

CORRINA. No no no. He's not.

ANGELO. How can you be so sure?

CORRINA. How can you be?

ANGELO. Because I have *faith*. Try it.

CORRINA. Alright as I am, thanks.

ANGELO (*points to the sky*). It might be a party. That's all I'm saying.

CORRINA. So we should all wait 'til we're dead to start living?

ANGELO. Not what I said. (*Beat.*) I live my life. This job is an investment so I can live it even better in the future. (*Beat.*) You want to be Captain yes?

CORRINA. …

ANGELO. Hey it's not a trick question. You like your job?

CORRINA. I love my job.

ANGELO. But you'll love it better when you're in charge. (*Beat.* ANGELO *grins.*) It's not so different, hey?

Five

The CAPTAIN *and* RIZAL *stand opposite one another.*

The CAPTAIN *sits. He gestures to one of the chairs.* RIZAL *sits down too, unhooking the satchel from his shoulder and placing it on his lap.*

CAPTAIN. Would you like a drink?

RIZAL. …

CAPTAIN. Tea, coffee. I've got some *elderflower* cordial. My wife introduced me to it.

RIZAL. I'm okay. Thank you.

Beat.

CAPTAIN. There's some biscuits I think?

RIZAL *shakes his head.*

RIZAL. Thank you. No.

Silence. RIZAL *taps his bag.*

Shall we?

CAPTAIN. Yes. Sure. Sure.

RIZAL *opens the satchel. He pulls out a small folding chess set.*

RIZAL *sets it out on the table between them carefully arranging all the pieces.*

You're going to thrash me again aren't you?

RIZAL. Oh. No, no. (*Beat.*) Maybe.

CAPTAIN. Secret champion.

RIZAL. Me? No. (*Beat.*) Do you know Eugene Torre?

CAPTAIN. Name seems familiar / is he deck or engine?

Beat. RIZAL *grins. He makes the first move.*

RIZAL. He's the *Grandmaster.*

CAPTAIN....

RIZAL. Best chess player in the Phillipines.

CAPTAIN. Ah. Right.

RIZAL. They put him in the world chess hall of fame.

CAPTAIN. Okay. It's a... *thing* then is it? Chess. In the Phillipines?

RIZAL. It's a thing, like, anywhere.

CAPTAIN. Got you.

RIZAL. You have this guy... Michael Adams. In Britain.

CAPTAIN. Do we? And he's a Grandmaster is he?

RIZAL. He's a Grandmaster. Yes.

CAPTAIN. You see... I *enjoy* it but I don't *follow* it. (*Beat.*) I'm not an expert. Like you.

RIZAL. At least you play.

CAPTAIN. Well I try. I'm *learning*, Rizal. Thanks to you.

CAPTAIN *ponders his move. He looks down to a piece then up at* RIZAL.

Should I?

RIZAL. Up to you, sir.

The CAPTAIN *makes the move. It's the wrong one.* RIZAL *takes the advantage. The* CAPTAIN *groans.*

We learn best by our mistakes.

CAPTAIN. Fair point.

Silence. They continue playing.

We have a female deck officer. Although you've probably already noticed that.

RIZAL. Yes, sir.

CAPTAIN. I hope everyone's behaving themselves.

RIZAL *stops, he looks up.*

The younger crew. Of course… I didn't mean *you.*

RIZAL. There are no problems, sir. Nothing I've seen.

CAPTAIN. Good. You'll let me know if there were?

RIZAL. Yes.

CAPTAIN. The first time I sailed with a woman she terrified the life out of me. Scared that if I talked too much to her she'd think I was a… lech and if I ignored her she'd think I was a rude bastard.

Silence. RIZAL *is concentrating on the game.*

Irina. Still remember her name… must be nearly thirty years ago, now. You can imagine what that was like. And she was… y'know…

The CAPTAIN *looks to* RIZAL *knowingly.*

RIZAL. Attractive?

Beat.

CAPTAIN. Yeah. (*Beat.*) She was very attractive.

Silence. RIZAL *is concentrating on the chess board.*

That was before I was married. So… it wouldn't have been /

RIZAL. You can't move the rook like that. Straight lines only.

CAPTAIN. Ah. Thank you.

RIZAL. And move your bishop first. Always you should be asking yourself, 'Does my move leave something unprotected?'

CAPTAIN. Yes.

The CAPTAIN *makes his move, he looks to* RIZAL. RIZAL *nods.*

Are you married, Rizal?

RIZAL. No.

CAPTAIN. Twenty-seven years. Get less for murder, hey?

RIZAL. Excuse me?

Beat.

CAPTAIN. It's erm / You wouldn't get as many years in prison if you killed someone.

RIZAL. You're not happy?

Beat.

CAPTAIN. No. No, I am. (*Beat.*) It's a joke.

Silence. RIZAL *nods.*

What else do you do? As a hobby.

RIZAL. I read. (*Beat, gesturing to the board again.*) Now your knight.

The CAPTAIN *looks down and moves the knight.*

CAPTAIN. You don't sing?

RIZAL. No. (*Beat.*) Not all Filipinos sing.

CAPTAIN. No. Of course not.

Silence.

RIZAL. Sir?

CAPTAIN. Yes?

RIZAL *makes his move.*

RIZAL. Checkmate.

Six

Night. CORRINA*'s cabin. She lies in bed, asleep. A thumping sound – it should seem as if it's coming from underneath the ship.*

CORRINA *jolts awake.*

The thumping sound morphs into the faint thud of music in the distance. CORRINA *puts on the light then gets out of bed. She pulls on her clothes and opens the door of her cabin.*

Walking into…

The crew room.

RAFAEL *is on the mic.* CORRINA *stands watching as he sings 'Rock Your Body' by Justin Timberlake.*

RAFAEL *sees* CORRINA *and stops singing, suddenly self-conscious.* ANGELO *rushes to* CORRINA.

ANGELO. Hey! You came to sing?

CORRINA. Oh God, no /

RAFAEL. You sing or you go. It's not a spectator sport.

RAFAEL *sits down.*

ANGELO. She's curious man, leave her.

RAFAEL. Teritoryo natin 'to. Opisyal siya. [This is our territory. She's an officer.]

CORRINA. Look, it's alright. I'll go.

ANGELO. No. It's fine. Stay.

RAFAEL. Gusto mo lang siyang kantutin. [You just want to fuck her.]

ANGELO. Ang bastos mo! Tumigil ka nga! [You're rude! Will you knock it off!]

CORRINA. Thought Justin Bieber had got on board, Rafael.

Had to come and check it out didn't I?

RAFAEL *scowls.* ANGELO *laughs.*

ANGELO. That's exactly who he wants to be. Justin Bieber.

RAFAEL. Fuck you. Anyway, it's Justin Timberlake.

CORRINA. Well I thought you were dead good.

Silence.

ANGELO. Man, take a compliment. (*Beat. To* CORRINA.) Hey! I got a song for you. I learnt it specially.

ANGELO *grabs the mic from* RAFAEL *and finds the track on the karaoke machine. The music starts.*

ANGELO *sings the second verse and chorus of 'Corrina, Corrina' by Ray Peterson.*

RAFAEL *turns the karaoke machine off.* CORRINA *claps and whistles.*

ANGELO. Your turn now!

CORRINA. No way.

ANGELO. Oh c'mon!

CORRINA. Absolutely not. I'm on watch now anyway.

ANGELO. I will have you singing by the end of this trip wait and see.

CORRINA. I very much doubt that, Angelo.

ANGELO. Nah you wait.

RIZAL *picks another track.*

RAFAEL. Hoy ako na! [Hey it's my turn!]

RIZAL. You walked away. [Umalis ka eh.]

CORRINA *exits as the music starts.*

RIZAL *sings 'Sumyaw, Sumunod' by The Boyfriends.*

Seven

Night-watch. The bridge. CORRINA *and* WILL*'s shift. They sit side by side at the control station.*

WILL. I pulled some strings.

CORRINA....

WILL. Get us on watch together. You were supposed to be with Danish Kris. Lovely bloke, boring as fuck. Send a glass eye to sleep.

CORRINA. Dodged a bullet then.

WILL. Defo mate, you owe me one.

Through the radio comes a series of shrieks and random insults followed by laughter and monkey sounds.

WILL. Channel sixteen.

CORRINA. How you s'posed to tell if anyone genuinely needs help with all that racket goin' on?

WILL. Shipping equivalent of knock down ginger, now. D'you ever play that when you were a kid?

CORRINA. Course.

WILL. Our favourite was this woman end of our street. Called it the witch's house. She had these *dolls* lined up on her window-sill. Loads and loads of fuckin'... dolls. Y'know those horrible Victorian ones in big velvet knickerbockers with real hair and massive eyes? Like a fuckin'... Stephen King film. Used to shout through her letterbox. One time she sticks a broom handle through, nearly takes me eye out. Threatened us with a knife once. Fuckin' crackers, she was.

CORRINA. We had Mr Spencer. Geography teacher. He had a breakdown and started camping in a tent in his living room. Always had bloodstains on the arse of his chinos. We'd go and bang on the window then he'd come out barefoot and chase us down the street screaming shit out of the bible.

WILL. Eyes on the screen.

Beat. CORRINA *looks back to the screen.*

WILL. He ever catch you?

CORRINA. Nah. He could barely stand up, poor fucker.

The radio crackles. A WOMAN*'s voice, incoherent.*

WILL. Oh 'ello. What d'you reckon? Dominatrix?

CORRINA. Definitely. Bit older. Bang into leather. She's got them kecks with the arse cut out.

WILL. Blonde?

CORRINA. Yeah. Two inch roots. Smokes like a chimney.

They listen again.

WILL. All talk, you can tell.

CORRINA. Nah. She'd have you for breakfast.

WILL. I'd be well up for that.

Beat. WILL *looks to* CORRINA. *She looks ahead.*

Finding your feet?

CORRINA. Yeah.

WILL. Making friends?

CORRINA. Dunno. I got thrown out of karaoke. Can't just watch, apparently.

WILL. Funny little fuckers them lot.

Beat.

CORRINA. Them lot?

WILL. Deck crew. Whatshisname… little… fuckin'… chatty one.

CORRINA. *Angelo.* (*Beat.*) He's alright. They're alright.

WILL. Most of them are, yeah. (*Beat.*) Very conscientious. (*Beat. Off* CORRINA.) What? They are. I'm not being /

CORRINA. Racist?

WILL. How's that racist? It's a positive thing. They are, they work hard. If that makes me racist /

CORRINA. They're alright. Angelo's nice. Friendly.

WILL. Very patronising.

CORRINA. I'm not generalising. I'm talking about a particular /

WILL. You ever been? Philippines?

CORRINA. No.

WILL. Beautiful country. Nice people. Hard working. And yeah… you're right they are very friendly. Every single one of them.

CORRINA. I said *he* was friendly. Not the entire nation.

WILL. And I'm saying you're right. He is. (*Beat.*) Bit too friendly sometimes.

CORRINA. What's that mean?

Beat.

WILL. Just keep your guard up, yeah?

CORRINA.…

WILL. Don't get too…

CORRINA. Too what?

WILL. It's a cultural thing innit? Some of them aren't used to a woman being… *open* with them /

CORRINA. Open?

WILL. Alright. Some of them aren't used to a woman full stop. Spend their whole lives on here. Surrounded by blokes. Suddenly they're figuring out how to live with one. S'not the same as us, is it? Going home after a couple of months. I'm not saying it's intentional. (*Beat.*) Gotta be assertive, Rina. Don't let them think they can walk all over you.

CORRINA. Doubt they think that. (*Beat.*) I can handle meself. Don't worry.

WILL. Still be saying that once we hit pirate waters will you?

CORRINA. Course.

WILL. Well if you need back-up when you're fronting it out with a machete wielding psycho /

CORRINA. Don't come to you?

WILL. Exactly.

CORRINA. Cheers.

WILL. Nah, got your back, mate, haven't I? (*Beat.*) Usually I have a bit of a laugh with a newbie. Sent the last cadet for a Bosun's punch.

CORRINA. I'm not a cadet.

WILL. Never said you were. (*Beat.*) He had a dead arm for two days. But I'll let you off.

CORRINA. I don't want any special treatment.

WILL. Not getting any, don't worry. (*Beat.*) Remember that time at Warsash when Fat Rob found a tampon in his curry?

CORRINA. 'Cause you put it there.

WILL. Dunno why he got so aggro, it was clean. (*Beat.*) You thought it was hilarious.

Beat.

CORRINA. I didn't. I thought it was fuckin' disgusting.

WILL. That why you pissed yourself for about three hours? (*Beat.*) Liar.

Silence.

Like you didn't do shit, anyway. What about that time you made me sit on that duff stool? Nearly broke me fuckin' back. Still get pain. Seen a specialist and he said I've damaged me nerves. Probably always be like that. (*Beat.*) I'm on prescription painkillers.

CORRINA. 'Cause of that?

WILL. Yeah.

Beat.

CORRINA. Fuck. (*Beat.*) I'm sorry.

WILL. Had to give up footy and everything. Have you not noticed me limping?

Silence.

Probably be in a wheelchair when I'm older.

CORRINA.…

WILL *bursts out laughing.*

Fuck off. Are you winding me up?

WILL. Course I'm winding you up, dickhead.

Silence.

Phoned you. Last summer. Still got the same number?

CORRINA. Yeah /

WILL. Left a couple of messages /

CORRINA. I know. Sorry. Did mean to call you back.

WILL. Wasn't making a big thing out of it. Kept popping in me head that's all. (*Beat.*) Thought about other things too. Haven't got a fucking… shrine or anything. Don't keep your photo in me wallet.

CORRINA (*mock offended*). Don't you?

WILL. No, it's on me dart board.

CORRINA. In your mum's house? (*Beat.*) Hang on… you don't actually still live at your mum's do you?

CORRINA *bursts out laughing.* WILL *flips her the middle finger.*

WILL. Saving for a deposit aren't I?

CORRINA. Right. Yeah.

WILL. *You* live with your mum. Alright for girls is it?

CORRINA. Don't live with me mum anymore. I live in a flat. Because I'm an adult.

WILL. I fuckin' hate you.

CORRINA. Hate you too.

Silence.

WILL. Anyone waiting for you?

CORRINA….

WILL. At home. A bloke. (*Pause.*) Sorry. None of my business. Being nosy.

Beat.

CORRINA. No. But I'm not / I don't want anything to happen.

WILL. How d'you mean?

CORRINA. On here… with anyone.

WILL. With me?

Beat.

CORRINA. Anyone. I'm not… looking for anything.

Beat. WILL *bursts out laughing.*

WILL. *Fuckin'* hell.

CORRINA. I just wanna be… upfront.

WILL. I say you pop in my head from time to time and you think I'm declaring undying fuckin' love. Tabs on yourself you, haven't you, mate? (*Beat.*) Only happened *once.*

CORRINA. I know /

WILL. How many years ago? Three, four?

CORRINA. I dunno. Three.

WILL. Three years ago. Tell you who else pops in my head from time to time. (*Beat.*) Fat fucking Rob. Now. Do I want to fuck fat Rob?

CORRINA. Okay, okay.

WILL. Just making conversation, mate.

CORRINA. Alright Jesus. Can we move on?

WILL. Forgot that about you.

CORRINA. Forgot what?

WILL. Intense, aren't you?

CORRINA. I'm not intense.

WILL. Fuckin' are.

CORRINA. How am I intense?

WILL. You're an INTP.

CORRINA....

WILL. Myers Briggs personality test. You ever done one?

CORRINA. No.

WILL. Ah mate, do it. Bet you fifty quid. INTP. Bill Gates is INTP... it's a good one. Massive overthinkers. Analyse everything. Attention to detail and all that. Suits being a captain INTP. (*Beat.*) I'm ESTP. Quick thinking but not a great planner. Instinctive, spontaneous. Bruce Willis is an ESTP. I'd do well in the army, me.

CORRINA. Right.

WILL. You should do one, Rina. (*Beat.*) Get to know yourself.

Beat.

CORRINA. Hate that by the way.

WILL. What?

CORRINA. *Rina.*

WILL. Always called you Rina, didn't I?

CORRINA. Yeah. And I hate it.

WILL. Why didn't you say?

CORRINA. I have said.

WILL. Really?

CORRINA. Yeah.

WILL. Then I *apologise*.

CORRINA. S'not a big deal.

WILL. If you *hate* it then it's a big deal, *Corrina*.

CORRINA. . . .

WILL. S'your name, it's important.

CORRINA. Thanks.

Beat. CORRINA *stands.*

WILL. What you doing?

CORRINA. Going to the loo.

WILL. Ask then. Don't just get up.

Beat. WILL *starts laughing.*

Your face. I fuckin' love it, mate.

CORRINA. Hysterical.

WILL. I'm sorry. (*Beat.*) You have my permission go to the toilet, Corrina.

Beat. CORRINA *leaves.* WILL *watches her go.*

Silence. The radio crackles, voices coming in and out.

Eight

Safety briefing. A map of the piracy zone on the wall. Next to it a large intricate plan of the ship. CORRINA *stands next to the* CAPTAIN *in front of the assembled crew*

CAPTAIN. This is a dangerous business we operate in. We lose two ships *every single day*. Collisions. Grounding. Sinking.

More than one and a half billion paid out in insurance every year. *Human behaviour* is at the root of virtually all that loss, *but* it's also the reason why the loss isn't greater. The capabilities and vulnerabilities of human beings will always be at the centre of our industry. Profits flow from safety, and without safety profits are hard to come by.

The devil and the deep blue sea. Look after *people* and profits will look after themselves. The welfare of your crewmembers is paramount.

A few murmurs from the CREW.

Okay. We're due to reach pirate waters in twenty-four hours. Let's all be crystal clear on protocol.

CAPTAIN *nods to* CORRINA *who reads from a clipboard.*

CORRINA. In the face of threats of attack by pirates, low manning levels are not likely to allow for sufficient lookouts to be deployed continuously in the danger areas, or to allow the crew to react effectively and in good time in the critical period when…

CORRINA *stops. A whispered argument is still taking place between* RAFAEL *and* ANGELO.

She catches ANGELO*'s eye and it stops.*

…an attack is threatened or underway. (*Beat.*) As we're aware, an attack is usually carried out using skiffs supported by mother ships. This tends to restrict their operations to moderate sea state. Sea states three and above are much more difficult for them, so keep conditions in mind while preparing for the piracy zone. (*Pause.*) The ship's speed is one of the most effective ways to prevent an attack. Sailing through high-risk waters we'll proceed at eighteen knots or as close as possible.

CAPTAIN. Engine room crew must be on top of this, we'll address them separately. Checks need to be increased threefold. We show no lights and we double the watch.

CORRINA *continues reading.*

CORRINA. It's vital to secure different entry points in the ship. Ensure no emergency exit can be opened from the outside. Pirates gaining access to the upper deck will be tenacious in their efforts to get to the accommodation section and in particular, the bridge. Doors and hatches providing access to bridge accommodation and machinery spaces should be properly secured. Prior to entering high-risk areas, procedures for controlling access to accommodation, machinery spaces and store-rooms should be set out and practiced.

CAPTAIN. We need to run daily drills. All defences need to be in proper working condition. Crew-members must know how to operate these during emergency situations.

CAPTAIN *gestures to* CORRINA *again. She reads.*

CORRINA. Anti-piracy laser, water cannon, anti-traction material for ships decking, razor wire canister, anti-piracy curtain, fire-hoses. Taser gun.

CORRINA *looks to the* CAPTAIN. *He nods for her to continue.*

The safety of the crew is of prime importance – we must ensure all measures are taken to prevent illegal boarding and external access to the ship's accommodation area. In the unlikely event that illegal boarding is successful, all crew must make their way immediately to the citadel which is located on the lower deck next to the medical bay. This is the ship's safe space, designed and constructed to resist forced entry. The whole concept of the citadel is –

WILL. Is the officer boring you?

WILL *is addressing* RAFAEL *who is yawning widely.* ANGELO *elbows him.*

What's your name?

RAFAEL. Rafael Santos.

WILL. Are you bored, Rafael Santos?

RAFAEL *shakes his head. He stands upright.*

I asked you a question?

RAFAEL *shakes his head.* WILL *looks to the* CAPTAIN.

CAPTAIN. I can guarantee it won't be *boring* if you find yourself in the middle of a hijacking situation.

RAFAEL *nods. Silence. The* CAPTAIN *gestures for* CORRINA *to continue.*

CORRINA. The whole concept of the citadel is lost if any crew-member is left outside before it is secured (*Beat.*) Last but by no means least. *Communication.* All crew-members must keep an active communication throughout. This means all personnel on duty to carry a radio, channel sixteen on in the bridge and the safe room. Identify the relevant emergency contact information available on the bridge. And make sure you *test* your communication equipment.

CAPTAIN. Are we all clear?

A few mutters from the CREW.

While you're at sea you are no longer what you were. You're not of your family, you're barely of your nation… you belong to your ship and your crew.

The CAPTAIN *leaves.* WILL *follows.*

RIZAL. Eighteen knots is a lie. The pirate skiff is *twenty-five* knots. They put up their ladders and cut through the razor wire. Easy.

CORRINA. Maybe you should do the safety briefing next time then.

RIZAL (*shrugs*). Pirates want to get on the ship. They get on the ship.

RAFAEL. I've been on this ship six months. He still doesn't know my fucking name. Won't even try to bluff it. (*Beat.*) I hate this guy.

ANGELO. Hate's a strong word.

RAFAEL. Pakyu, Angelo. Fuck you and your sister.

ANGELO. Which one?

RAFAEL. Acts like he's God. He's a fucking bus driver. (*Beat.*) And we're meant to bow to him?

ANGELO. If he's a bus driver what does that make us?

RAFAEL. Fleas on the seats.

ANGELO. Extremely hardworking fleas.

CORRINA. Okay listen, I need to allocate crew members for the safety drills –

RAFAEL. I yawn because I work twenty hours in a day. You keep me still and talk at me for hours my eyelids gonna close, especially when you tell me the same shit I heard fifty times or more. Yes I find it boring. Fucking *kupal*.

RIZAL. We are in God's hands.

CORRINA. Okay /

RAFAEL. That means he just sits back and let's shit happen.

RIZAL. And you complain when the coast is clear.

CORRINA. Is anyone listening?

RAFAEL. Maybe it wouldn't even be so bad. I heard about a ship, hijacked by Somalians. They brought their own cook. The crew ate better than they had in *months*. And the Somalis share their drugs. They have an endless supply.

CORRINA. Well if you don't pay attention your wish might come true, Rafael.

RAFAEL. Good food and drugs all day long. They just sit there guarding their hostages eating and getting high. One day I might be a pirate.

CORRINA. Okay. Enough now.

ANGELO. Yeah c'mon.

RIZAL. One day I might punch you in the face.

ANGELO. You won't do that.

RIZAL. Watch me.

CORRINA (*shouting*). Shut the fuck up!

Silence.

Daily drills. We need to look at the rota –

RAFAEL *stares at* CORRINA. *He mutters something in Filipino under his breath and laughs.* CORRINA *stops, suddenly self-conscious.*

ANGELO. Have some respect.

CORRINA. If you've got something to say just speak up. I can't hear you properly.

RAFAEL *is silent.*

ANGELO. He was making a joke.

RAFAEL *hits* ANGELO *on the arm.*

CORRINA. About me?

RAFAEL. No.

CORRINA. I love a joke. Go on.

Silence.

I'm waiting. (*Beat.*) Stand here all fucking day if I have to.

RAFAEL. It was nothing.

Silence.

CORRINA. I'll share some of my favourites then shall I?

ANGELO. Sure. We like jokes.

CORRINA. Great. Why is life like a penis?

Silence.

Because women make it hard for no reason.

Pause. CORRINA *fronts it out.*

Is Google male or female? (*Beat.*) Female. 'Cause it won't let you finish a sentence without making a suggestion. (*Beat.*) Man driving a car hits a woman. Whose fault is it? The man's obviously. What's he doing, driving in the kitchen? (*Beat.*) Go on Rafael.

Beat. WILL *appears.*

WILL. What's happening?

CORRINA. It's okay /

RAFAEL. It wasn't *that* kind of joke.

WILL. What kind of joke?

RAFAEL *mutters something.*

In *English.*

RAFAEL. It's not your business.

WILL. Excuse me?

RAFAEL. You weren't here. I didn't do anything.

CORRINA. I was trying to talk through the rota /

WILL. And you were being disrespectful?

RAFAEL. No.

WILL. That's what it sounds like.

CORRINA. I'm dealing with it /

WILL. Apologise.

RAFAEL. What for?

WILL. Apologise.

Beat.

RAFAEL. No.

WILL. Pardon?

RAFAEL. I didn't do anything.

WILL. I'll count to three.

RAFAEL. This is bullshit.

WILL. What did you say?

Beat.

RAFAEL. I said it's fucking bullshit.

A beat before WILL *lunges at* RAFAEL *and swipes his face. He grabs him and pushes him up against the wall with force.*

CORRINA *looks on in shock.* ANGELO *rushes to* RAFAEL.

ANGELO. Hey hey hey!

WILL *holds* RAFAEL *by the scruff of the neck.* CORRINA *stands back shocked.*

RAFAEL. I'm sorry.

WILL. To Officer Wilkinson not me.

RAFAEL *looks to* CORRINA *who is rooted to the spot.*

CORRINA. Let go of him.

WILL *stares at* CORRINA *then let's go of* RAFAEL.

RAFAEL (*to* CORRINA, *reluctantly*). I'm sorry.

WILL *lets go.*

WILL. Get out. (*Beat.*) All of you.

RAFAEL *rushes out,* ANGELO *and* RIZAL *following behind.* CORRINA *is speechless.*

A thank you wouldn't go amiss?

CORRINA. Thank you for *what?*

WILL. Just leave you next time then is it, yeah?

WILL *stares at* CORRINA.

Told you, mate. Didn't I? (*Beat.*) Gotta nip that shit in the bud.

Nine

The crew room. ANGELO, RAFAEL *and* RIZAL *sitting together eating.* CORRINA *enters holding a tray of food. She takes a seat at a table on her own.*

After a few moments ANGELO *comes to join her. He gestures to the empty chair.*

ANGELO. Is anybody sitting here?

CORRINA. Not unless they're very very small, Angelo.

ANGELO. It's okay if I join you?

CORRINA. Sure.

ANGELO *sits.*

ANGELO. Filipina women never eat alone.

CORRINA. I'm not Filipina.

ANGELO. At home anyone eating on their own is like… something *bad* has happened, man. People pity you.

CORRINA. Right.

ANGELO. It's like you're an outcast.

CORRINA. I get it. Thanks.

ANGELO. Some of them can be stupid.

CORRINA *nods. She carries on eating.*

Are you upset?

CORRINA. I work on ships, Angelo. Takes more than that.

RAFAEL *looks over and mutters in Filipino.*

RAFAEL. Traydor. [Traitor.]

ANGELO. Wala siyang kasalanan [It's not her fault]

RAFAEL. Talaga [Really?]

Silence.

ANGELO. These things happen. Fighting, lots of anger. (*Whispers*) I'm not a violent person but sometimes I say yeah, man you deserved that. Or I think it to myself at least. It's not usually a good thing to speak your mind.

ANGELO *rolls up his sleeve and points to a small scar.*

Can you see this?

CORRINA *peers at his arm.*

This was a cook five years ago. (*Beat.*) It's like three minutes tops for noodles yeah? He had them in the pan half an hour. Always like jelly. By the time we get to the Suez Canal I can't take it anymore. I ask him not to over-boil the noodles and he stabs me with a fork.

CORRINA. Harsh. What did you do about it?

ANGELO. I stopped complaining about the food.

RAFAEL *starts muttering.* CORRINA *looks up at him.*

It's like little schoolboys or something. A lot of… testosterone. They don't know how to be. (*Beat.*) I have five sisters. Two daughters. They all teach me about respect. I'm not scared of women. I can talk to women much better, share stuff. I can't talk to these people, not really.

RAFAEL. Angelo, why is she in our room? This is *our* space.

ANGELO. Shut up, Rafael.

CORRINA. I'm just eating my food.

RAFAEL. And spying on us? To go and tell your boyfriend?

CORRINA. What you talking about?

RAFAEL *turns his back.*

ANGELO. Ignore him. He's angry because you got us a warning /

CORRINA. *I* didn't get you a warning /

ANGELO. You know what I mean.

CORRINA. Angelo, this is bullshit.

ANGELO. Hey hey. It's nothing. Rafael he's just a little... *fuck.*

RAFAEL *spins around.*

RAFAEL. What did you say?

ANGELO. Yeah. I called you a little fuck, man. Because you're a little fuck sometimes.

RAFAEL *picks up a handful of mashed potato and throws it at* ANGELO. *It hits him on the side of the face.* RIZAL *carries on reading.* RAFAEL *laughs and bangs the table.*

Ano ka ba! [What are you like!?]

ANGELO *wipes potato from his face, humiliated.*

School boys. My kids are more mature than these people. Para 'tong tanga. [You're acting stupid!]

RAFAEL. Angelo calm down man, I'm trying to eat in peace.

WILL *stands by the door unseen. He watches as* CORRINA *takes a napkin and wipes some of the potato from* ANGELO*'s cheek.*

Aw, you're being looked after by your girlfriend, Angelo! Ang kyut kyut niyo naman! [You're so cute!]

CORRINA. Are you jealous, Rafael? (*Beat.*) When was the last time you were even with a woman anyway? And I don't mean one you paid for.

RAFAEL *stands and walks out.* CORRINA *watches him go and notices* WILL *in the doorway for the first time.*

WILL *stares at her for a moment then leaves.*

Ten

CORRINA*'s cabin. She is sleeping. Background noise of karaoke can be heard.*

The thumping noise again then the presence of a figure in the room, a large shadow looming across the wall.

CORRINA *sits bolt upright as the light suddenly goes on.*

WILL *is standing there. He is holding a bag in his arms.*

WILL. Rina. Wake up, get up. Quick.

CORRINA *comes to, shocked by* WILL*'s presence.*

C'mon. Get up.

CORRINA. What?

WILL. They're here. They're fucking here, mate.

CORRINA. Who? What the fuck's going on?

WILL. Skiffs behind the ship. About four of them.

CORRINA *stares confused.*

Pirates. They're getting their ladders out. They're getting on board. Hurry up.

CORRINA. Where's the alarm? I didn't hear /

WILL. Are you fucking serious? It's been going for the past ten minutes. Corrina, we've got to go *now.*

CORRINA *tumbles out of bed. Pulling a jumper on over her pyjamas.* WILL *stands by the door and they both run out, making their way to the citadel – a small sparse room on the lower deck.*

CORRINA *crouches in the corner, her arms wrapped tightly around herself.*

WILL *locks the door behind them. He puts the keys in his pocket.*

CORRINA. What happens now?

WILL. I dunno.

Beat.

CORRINA. Has this ever… have you ever had this before?

WILL *shakes his head. He paces.*

WILL. You ever meet Dan Phillips?

Beat. CORRINA *shakes her head.*

Couple of years above us at Warsash. Sailed with him last year. On watch one night and they got ambushed from both sides, no time to hide or do fuck all. He legs it down onto the deck and a fuckin' massive hook comes over the side… a whole line of them climbing up the rope, machetes between their teeth. He's got this axe and he just starts clobbering them… blood everywhere but they're hanging on, then he hears this noise behind and there's a whole other line of the cunts /

CORRINA. Stop it. Please stop it.

WILL *bends down. He puts his arms around* CORRINA.

WILL. Come on. It's alright. You're okay. They can't get us in here.

WILL *holds* CORRINA. *They stay like this.*

CORRINA. I can't hear anything? Can you hear anything?

WILL *stands he goes to the door and listens out.*

WILL. No.

CORRINA. What about everyone else?

WILL. Probably locked themselves in their cabins.

CORRINA. How do we get out? We're trapped. They'll take over the ship.

WILL. Flares have gone out… there'll be people on the way.

CORRINA. We're hostages.

WILL. They'll send people, they'll send the military

CORRINA growing increasingly panicked, she tries to catch a breath.

Hey hey hey… You're alright. It's okay. Got to try and keep calm.

CORRINA. How can I keep calm?

WILL. They can't get in here. It's like Fort Knox. There's no way. (*Beat.*) You gotta focus yeah? Work on your breathing, keep talking. C'mon… talk to me.

CORRINA. I can't / my mind's blank.

WILL. Tell us stuff about home.

CORRINA. Don't wanna talk about home.

WILL. Anything then.

CORRINA. Why aren't you freaking out?

WILL. I am freaking out I'm just good at hiding it.

CORRINA. You talk then.

WILL. Okay /

CORRINA. What was that? Can you hear anything?

WILL. Rina, relax.

CORRINA. How can I / how can I relax?

WILL. Breathe. You're alright.

She nods, rubbing her hands on her face.

That's it. (*Beat.*) Got a little admirer there haven't you?

CORRINA. What?

WILL. *Angelo.*

Beat.

CORRINA. No.

WILL. Yes, mate.

Silence.

Come on.

CORRINA. Come on what?

WILL. Chat to me. Fuck's sake, mate… it's like getting shit off a blanket /

CORRINA. I'm *frightened.*

WILL *reaches into his bag and pulls out a flask. He throws it* CORRINA.

What is it?

WILL. Vodka.

CORRINA. Is that a good idea? Need to be sharp.

WILL *gestures for her to throw it back.*

WILL. Only thing I need to be if I'm getting a machete in my head is absolutely fucking wasted but you do you, mate.

CORRINA *opens the flask and takes a huge gulp, coughing as she swallows. She hands it back to* WILL.

You do wanna be careful though y'know? (*Beat.*) Won't do yourself any favours. Giving them mixed messages.

Pause. Off CORRINA*'s confusion.*

I'm sticking up for you… giving out warnings. Next thing you're in their mess, all over fucking… Angelo. Giving him ideas.

CORRINA. What?

WILL. They don't need much encouragement, mate, trust me. (*Beat.*) Doesn't give you much of a case either does it? If anything happens.

WILL *takes another swig. Pause.*

CORRINA. Can we try and figure out what the fuck we're gonna do here?

WILL. You're the safety officer. You tell me.

Silence. CORRINA *stares at* WILL *as he takes another sip of vodka then offers the flask back over to her.*

CORRINA. Did you see anybody else?

WILL....

CORRINA. Before you came to me. Did you see anyone, talk to anybody?

WILL. Just come straight to you.

CORRINA. There was nobody else heading here.

WILL. No.

CORRINA. That seems a bit weird.

WILL. They'll have barricaded themselves in their cabins won't they?

CORRINA. What about the Captain?

WILL. What? D'you think this is like the Titanic? He's gonna be leading the charge like some noble hero? He'll be fuckin' shitting in a bucket now, mate.

CORRINA *stands. She goes to the door and leans against it to listen.*

CORRINA. I can't hear anything. (*Beat.*) How come it's just us two?

WILL. Told you. I dunno.

CORRINA. Nobody else thought to come down here?

WILL. Obviously not.

Silence. CORRINA *stares at* WILL.

What?

CORRINA. Open the door.

WILL. Are you fucking mad?

CORRINA. Open the door, please.

WILL. There's psychos out there ready to chop your head off.

CORRINA. Open it.

Silence. CORRINA *stares. She knows.*

WILL. Fuck.

WILL *covers his mouth, laughing.*

I'm sorry. I'm so fucking / It was meant to be… fuck, I'm sorry. (*Beat.*) Got to admit that was a good one though?

CORRINA. Open the fucking door now.

WILL. Look I misjudged it… took it a bit far. I'm sorry.

Silence. WILL *holds a hand out to* CORRINA. *She stays put.*

CORRINA. Why?

WILL.…

CORRINA. Why would you do that?

WILL. Mate. I swear… I didn't even think you'd fall for it.

Silence.

CORRINA. Can I go now?

WILL. Of course. Fucking hell mate. I genuinely /

CORRINA. Can you open the door then?

WILL. I'm a dickhead. I'm so sorry.

CORRINA. Can you open the door?

WILL. Are you alright?

CORRINA. Yeah can you open the door?

WILL. Mate. Calm down.

CORRINA. I'm calm. Open the door.

WILL. Can you just… give us a minute. One minute, that's all.

Silence.

Have I done anything to piss you off.

Silence.

Apart from this. (*Laughing.*) I mean, fucking hell… this backfired… but I mean generally… have I… pissed you off? (*Beat.*) Because it feels like there's this… *distance* or something. Like… it's not what it used to be.

CORRINA. What's not what it used to be?

WILL. You and me.

Silence.

CORRINA. Open the door.

WILL. I'm trying to chat to you. As mates.

CORRINA. You're not my mate.

WILL. I get that you're pissed off. I fuckin'… haven't made this easy have I? I'm not excusing myself. It was a stupid joke. But part of it was wanting to just be alone. And talk.

CORRINA. I don't want to talk.

WILL. Last time I saw you. It was that night wasn't it? And I thought we had a nice time. Then you blank me. Completely fucking blanked me an' you know what mate if that was the other way round, I'd be getting called all the cunts going and you'd have a point but I wouldn't do that /

CORRINA. I said no.

WILL.…

CORRINA. That night. I said no. And you carried on. (*Beat.*) I told you to stop.

Silence.

WILL. Fuckin' hell.

Silence.

That is / that's the sort of shit that… *ends* people that is. Fucking accusations like that.

CORRINA *goes for the keys in* WILL*'s pocket. He grabs them and hold them in the air.*

I haven't finished.

CORRINA. I have. Let me out.

WILL. You can't come out with that *shit* and then just leave. What the fuck, Corrina?

CORRINA. Let me go.

WILL *dodges* CORRINA *as she reaches desperately for the keys.*

Let me out. Let me out. Let me out. (*Beat.*) LET ME FUCKING OUT NOW!

CORRINA *rushes to the door,* WILL *blocks it. She charges at him but he holds her arms tightly.*

A noise from the corner of the room and ANGELO *appears.*

ANGELO. Let her go, man.

CORRINA *stops still,* WILL *stares in shock but maintains his grip on* CORRINA.

She wants to get out. (*Beat.*) Take your hands off her and let her go. I mean it.

WILL *lets go.*

WILL. Just having a laugh, mate.

ANGELO. Open the door.

WILL *opens the door.* CORRINA *exits.*

She runs back to her cabin, locking the door behind her after she enters. For a moment CORRINA *stands perfectly still before suddenly the room tilts dramatically.*

A storm.

The drawers of a cupboard fly open. CORRINA *falls against the berth. It tilts the other way books and an alarm clock fly off a shelf, a bowl smashes onto the floor.*

The swell of the waves increases violently. CORRINA *clings on.*

ACT TWO

One

CORRINA *stands by the door in the* CAPTAIN*'s office.*

CAPTAIN. Come in, come in… Sit down. Take a seat.

CORRINA *sits*

CAPTAIN. Bad night last night.

CORRINA.…

CAPTAIN. The weather.

CORRINA. Yes, Sir.

CAPTAIN. Worst one I ever knew was a force eleven. Waves nearly forty feet high. I'm not a religious man but I said a prayer that night. (*Beat.*) How did you sleep?

CORRINA. Not very well.

CAPTAIN. I've got a trick. Might not work for everyone but it's worth sharing. First complete darkness… got to block out all the light. Then you need to go with the flow of the ship's roll, don't push against it or try and hang on. (*Beat.*) Re-align your body like you're in a cradle. Let the sea be your mother, baby in the womb sort of feeling. It's a state of mind more than anything. Like trying not to tense up to break a fall. Easier said than done but everything's so much better when you just… relax and go with the flow. (*Beat.*) Give it a go.

CORRINA. Thank you.

CAPTAIN. How are you?

Beat.

CORRINA. I'm… okay.

CAPTAIN. Good.

CORRINA. I'm not trying to cause trouble.

CAPTAIN. Nobody's suggesting that. (*Beat.*) What did I say? That door is always open.

CORRINA. Thank you.

CAPTAIN. Communication is key. Onboard ship it's essential. (*Beat.*) Do you know how many disputes I've had to resolve over the years. Grudges, ongoing feuds… physical violence? I'm not suggesting for a moment that people shouldn't be held accountable but my priority is ensuring that we always move *forward*.

Silence. There's a knock at the door.

Come in.

The door opens and WILL *enters.*

Come in. Hello. Grab a chair.

WILL. Hello, Sir.

CORRINA *stares.* WILL *nods towards her.*

WILL *picks up a chair and sits down next to* CORRINA *opposite the* CAPTAIN.

CAPTAIN. I thought perhaps it'd be a good idea to… *open up* the dialogue. Think of me as HR. Forget about hierarchies. (*Pause.*) Who would like to begin?

CORRINA.…

WILL. If I could start by offering an apology to Officer Wilkinson for any misunderstanding /

CAPTAIN. Perhaps it would be / excuse me for interrupting but perhaps it would be more appropriate for Officer Wilkinson to speak first?

WILL. Sure. Yes. Sorry.

CAPTAIN. Officer Wilkinson would you like to start?

Beat.

CORRINA. I don't. (*Beat.*) Sorry.

CAPTAIN. Take your time.

Silence. CORRINA *is in fight or flight.*

Could you explain your concerns?

CORRINA. Sir. (*Beat.*) I didn't expect that… the officer… would be present. This is /

I can't… (*Pause.*) I don't want to do this.

CAPTAIN. I don't think any of us want to be doing this.

CORRINA. I was under the impression this was confidential. It's a formal comp /

CAPTAIN. The best way to move forwards, working and living in such close proximity, is to discuss it openly in a *safe space.*

CORRINA. That's my / This doesn't feel like…

CAPTAIN. Like what?

CORRINA. Safe /

CAPTAIN. You're perfectly /

WILL. Jesus / You're safe. Sorry, Sir.

The CAPTAIN *raises a hand towards* WILL.

CAPTAIN. You're perfectly safe. (*Beat.*) I've always found it much more efficient to air grievances this way. Face to face.

Silence. The CAPTAIN *gestures to* CORRINA.

Please go ahead.

CORRINA.…

CAPTAIN. The incident in question?

WILL. Captain, I feel as though I should /

The CAPTAIN *raises a hand and gestures towards* CORRINA.

Sorry.

Pause.

CORRINA. I want to change my watch.

CAPTAIN. Can you elaborate.

Beat.

CORRINA. Officer Davis came into my cabin last night and informed me that we were under attack from pirate skiffs. (*Beat.*) We went down to the citadel and he locked the door /

WILL. Sir /

The CAPTAIN *raises his hand towards* WILL. *He nods for* CORRINA *to continue.*

CORRINA. Obviously I was very frightened. (*Beat.*) After a while he confessed that there was no hijack taking place and that he had lied. Then he refused to open the door and let me out.

Pause.

CAPTAIN. Is that all you want to say for the moment?

Beat. CORRINA *nods.*

CAPTAIN. Office Davis. You may speak now.

WILL. I did take Officer Wilkinson to the citadel under false pretences. I admit that. (*Beat.*) I'd like to explain my reasons.

Silence. The CAPTAIN *nods.*

I have concerns about Officer Wilkinson's mental state /

CORRINA. Sir, that's not true /

CAPTAIN. Please let Officer Davis speak.

CORRINA. But that isn't /

CAPTAIN. This is his turn to talk.

CAPTAIN *nods to* WILL.

WILL. So… yeah I've been concerned.

CAPTAIN. Concerned about what, exactly?

WILL. Officer Wilkinson told me that she had taken time out because of mental health issues which of course is /

CORRINA. That's not what I said /

WILL. Not a problem /

CAPTAIN. Officer Wilkinson, I'm not going to ask again.

Silence. CAPTAIN *nods to* WILL.

WILL. I've noticed some… erratic behaviour resulting in some mistakes while on duty.

CORRINA. That's a lie /

WILL. Then last night… I found Officer Wilkinson had been drinking. I took her to the citadel to sober up.

CORRINA. Sir, that's not true.

CAPTAIN. Final warning.

WILL. She was intoxicated and shouting so I did lock the door. And I apologise for that. I just wanted to contain the situation. (*Beat.*) I gave her an unofficial warning and she became very angry. After a few minutes I opened the door and she left.

Silence.

CORRINA *is shaken, reeling.*

CORRINA. Sir, did you speak to Angelo… the member of deck crew? He witnessed the whole thing? (*Beat.*) Angelo Andrada.

The CAPTAIN *is bemused now. He looks to* WILL. WILL *is impassive.*

WILL. He did, Sir.

CORRINA. So he should be here too. This feels / Officer Davis let himself into my cabin when I was asleep.

WILL. No.

CORRINA *is growing increasingly upset.*

CORRINA. You *did* / why are you saying that? Sir, he did. He told me the ship was under attack then he locked me / he locked me in the citadel. Without my consent. He had vodka with him and he *gave* it to me. I was terrified. I thought we might die. Then… when I realised it wasn't true he physically restrained me /

WILL. No.

CORRINA. I don't… this is all lies, Sir. (*Beat.*) Angelo saw it, he saw everything. I'd really / if he could be here now then he'd tell you himself?

Beat.

WILL. He *was* a witness, Sir.

Pause. The CAPTAIN *nods.*

CAPTAIN. Okay.

The CAPTAIN *stands and leaves the room.*

CORRINA *and* WILL *sit in silence. It's excruciating.*

CORRINA. Why are you doing this to me?

WILL. It's probably best we wait until the Captain comes back in.

Silence.

CORRINA. Why would you want to do this?

WILL. I don't want to speak without the Captain present.

CORRINA. Trying to fucking ruin me.

WILL. You've got a cheek.

Silence. CORRINA *in disbelief.*

After another minute or so the CAPTAIN *returns. He sits back down.*

CAPTAIN. On his way.

Silence.

CORRINA. Sir /

CAPTAIN. Let's wait shall we?

Silence. The tension is palpable.

After a few more moments there's a knock at the door.

Come in.

ANGELO *enters, in work overalls, covered in grease and paint.*

He nods to the CAPTAIN, *avoiding eye contact with* CORRINA.

Angelo.

ANGELO. Captain. Sir.

CAPTAIN. We won't keep you. I know you're busy.

ANGELO. It's no problem, Sir.

Beat.

CAPTAIN. Angelo. Will you give your account of what happened yesterday between the two officers present?

ANGELO. In the citadel?

CAPTAIN. Yes.

Beat. ANGELO *looks towards* CORRINA.

ANGELO. Now, Captain?

CAPTAIN. Now, please.

Silence.

ANGELO. I saw… Officer Davis and Officer Wilkinson… talking.

CAPTAIN. Talking?

Beat.

ANGELO. Arguing.

CAPTAIN. About what?

ANGELO. The lady / Officer Wilkinson wanted him to open the door. And he / Officer Davis was saying no. She was getting very angry. He was trying to calm her down.

CAPTAIN. Did he physically restrain her?

Beat.

ANGELO. No.

CORRINA. That's not true /

CAPTAIN. Did it appear to you that Officer Wilkinson had been drinking alcohol.

Pause.

ANGELO. She had vodka yes. Bottle of vodka. (*Beat.*) She was drunk.

CORRINA. No!

CAPTAIN. You specifically asked for this member of crew to be present to give his account. Let him speak. (*Beat. To* ANGELO.) Please continue.

Beat.

ANGELO. Officer Davis was saying… erm, Officer Wilkinson… she has to calm down and stop shouting… that she cannot behave like this.

Pause. ANGELO *still avoiding eye contact.*

CAPTAIN. What happened then?

Beat. ANGELO *stares ahead.*

ANGELO. More shouting. More anger from Officer Wilkinson. Then Officer Davis opened the door and she / Officer Wilkinson left.

Beat.

CAPTAIN. What were you doing in there, Angelo?

Beat.

ANGELO. In the citadel?

CAPTAIN. Yes. Why were you there?

Beat.

ANGELO. I was… checking, Sir.

CAPTAIN. Checking what?

Beat.

WILL. I'd asked Angelo to do an audit on supplies, Sir. Water, first aid… I didn't realise he'd be in there at that exact moment but I did ask him previously.

Silence. The CAPTAIN *nods.*

CAPTAIN. Is there anything else you want to add? (*Beat.*) About what you saw?

ANGELO. No, Sir.

Beat.

CAPTAIN. Then please… get back to your work. Thank you… Angelo.

ANGELO. Thank you, Sir.

CORRINA *stares ahead as* ANGELO *as he exits, head bowed.*

Silence.

CAPTAIN. Officer Wilkinson? (*Beat.*) Is there anything you want to say in response?

Silence.

Nothing you want to say?

Pause.

CORRINA. No. There's nothing I want to say.

Silence.

CAPTAIN. If you'd been drinking on duty obviously that would be instant dismissal. (*Beat.*) Bearing in mind your emotional issues that have been outlined in this meeting, I'm prepared to let this go with a verbal warning. On condition there is reparation made in the form of an apology to Officer Davis.

Silence.

Officer Wilkinson?

Beat.

CORRINA. An apology?

CAPTAIN. Yes.

Silence.

Otherwise a formal written warning will be recorded in the logbook. (*Beat.*) I'd think carefully about that if I were you.

Long silence.

CORRINA. I'm sorry.

Beat. WILL *nods.*

WILL. Apology accepted.

Beat.

CAPTAIN. I'll also have to rethink some aspects of your role for the time being. Officer Davis and I can discuss that.

Silence.

Okay. (*Beat.*) Let's put this behind us and move forward with grace then shall we?

Two

CORRINA*'s cabin. She pulls off her uniform and throws it on the floor.*

CORRINA *sits on the bed, in a T-shirt and jogging bottoms, her uniform is now hanging on the back of the door. A small tray of food in front of her. She picks at it before removing the tray and sliding it under the berth.*

She pulls the covers over her head.

Darkness. The long low repetitive thumping noise morphing into…

The sound of music – karaoke.

CORRINA *sits up slams on the light. She stands and opens her cupboard pulling out the bottle of vodka. She opens it and takes a sip.*

Then another. Then another.

She lies back down.

Darkness.

In CORRINA*'s dream, large shadows play against the wall. There's an eerie underwater quality to her cabin. She wakes up thinking she's drowning, gasping for air.*

Karaoke in the background again.

CORRINA *dances in her cabin.*

She lies on the floor.

Light pours in. Morning.

CORRINA *wakes. Slowly, she gets dressed into overalls. Her officer's uniform still hanging on the back of her door.*

Three

The upper deck. CORRINA *is removing rust from metal pillars.*

ANGELO *appears.*

CORRINA *ignores him.*

ANGELO. That's not your job.

Silence.

Hey. That's not your job.

CORRINA. It is now.

Silence. ANGELO *stays put watching her.*

Fuck d'you want, Angelo?

Beat.

ANGELO. I'm sorry.

CORRINA. Right.

ANGELO. I had no choice.

Silence.

You know I'm a good guy.

CORRINA *stops and looks at him.*

I have daughters.

CORRINA. Fuck. Sorry. I *forgot*. You've got *daughters*. You're practically a *woman*. (*Beat.*) Jesus. Okay, now fuck off.

ANGELO. What can I do?

CORRINA. You can go and knock on the Captain's door and tell him the fucking truth.

Beat.

ANGELO. If I speak out they sack me. It's simple.

CORRINA. They can't *sack* you for that.

ANGELO. Yes they can. *Especially* for that. You think blacklists don't exist?

CORRINA. I think you're a fake and a people pleaser and a weak weak man, Angelo.

ANGELO. No /

CORRINA. Yes. I had respect for you but you're a coward. My dad was the same. (*Beat.*) He never even set foot on a fucking ship. (*Beat.*) He was in prison. Came out. Went back in again. Over and over. (*Beat.*) It was what he wanted us to think. That he was having *adventures*. (*Beat.*) What's that thing they say about seafarers? Either liars or wankers. Or both.

Silence.

ANGELO. I hurt you. I'm very sorry.

CORRINA. You didn't hurt *me*, Angelo. Fucking hell… you think you have the power to hurt me? You're being *exploited*. Your kids don't even know you. Your wife lives in another country. What happened to ten years and stopping?

ANGELO. I do it for them. I try to be the person they think I am. Somebody to be proud of.

CORRINA. Can I tell you something, Angelo? They don't think anything of you. (*Beat.*) How can they? They don't even know you.

ANGELO. Neither do you.

CORRINA. Clearly not.

ANGELO. If you did then you wouldn't say those things. About my family. You don't know my family. You don't know my life.

Beat.

CORRINA. No. I don't.

Silence.

What were you really doing in the citadel? Don't tell me you were checking fuckin' supplies.

ANGELO. I was sleeping. (*Beat.*) Please don't tell the Captain. A human being cannot work these hours. It's impossible. We go in turns. An hour here, an hour there. Set our alarm. (*Beat.*) Rafael can't be trusted. He keeps hitting snooze. (*Beat.*) But it's the only way. No sleep is *dangerous*.

CORRINA. There's laws. Rules about shift lengths, breaks.

ANGELO. For *you*. Yes. He gives that big speech, the Captain. Makes him look good. Makes him feel good. It's all bullshit. Hawak n'ya ang pera. [He holds the money.] (ANGELO *rubs his fingers together to indicate cash*.) Profits. (*Beat*.) Everything is money, no? And we're trapped.

CORRINA. I'm not trapped.

ANGELO. No?

Silence.

You want to know the worst thing I ever heard in my life? (*Beat*.) I'm working on the ship, another ship, and I'm talking with this guy Mico, also from the Phillipines. I don't know him but he knows some of the people I know and we get on and I feel like I can talk to him. Not like it is with Rafael and Rizal, all shouting and jokes. Talking about real things. (*Beat*.) Like I can talk to you. And I'm feeling low because I miss everyone, I miss my family. So I tell him… I tell him I'm homesick. And he says 'Angelo, *this* is your home. Right here.' He meant it to be nice but it was the worst thing I ever heard in my life.

CORRINA. Leave then.

ANGELO. I can't. There's people. Back home. (*Beat*.) I owe them money.

CORRINA. What people?

ANGELO. Bad people. Loan sharks. (*Beat*.) I started on this ship eight months ago. At first it's fine. I get my wages first month but the second month I'm waiting and nothing's happening. (*Beat*.) For Rafael and Rizal it's not a problem. They get their money on the ship. Cash. Straight from the Captain's hand. Mine gets sent to my family. A lot of crew prefer it this way except for the fact that it's always delayed. (*Beat*.) I got my mother-in-law struggling, looking after the children and my wife isn't earning enough to cover it all but part of me thinks, this is good, this is a way to save, they have to pay me three months in one go now. We make it go further. Maybe even save some. Hangga't makitid ang kumot, matutong mamaluktot. That's what she says, my wife. While the blanket is short, learn how to bend, yeah? Then it's the fourth month. I call the company and they say it's been a *glitch*… man they love that word.

Glitch.

It's a *glitch* with the system. But they're fixing it, it's getting sorted, it's going to be okay soon. Now it's three months and I'm desperate and I can't chase it up because I'm in the middle of the fucking sea, excuse me. I can't think straight. I start to panic.

Someone gives me a number.

A woman in Quezon city called Angelica. She has a business helping out Filipino's abroad. Lending money. (*Beat.*) Man I'm not a fool. I know about loan sharks. But she's a *woman*. And this guy told me, she just does this by herself… it's almost like a charity thing. I know what you're thinking…

I call her and she is so nice and funny and makes a joke about our names being the same. Voice like honey and she treats it all like, 'Angelo, it's one of those things, you have no idea how many times I get this call. It's simple. I lend you the money when you get paid you give it back with a little interest, I have to make a living, and we're square.'

And I think… it's only for a little while.

The money goes in and I can breathe out. I'm still chasing my wages but I can breathe. We dock in Singapore and I go shopping to get my kids presents. I go a little bit crazy because I know it won't last long but I'm thinking of their faces like it's Christmas.

Four days later it's all gone.

I miss Angelica's first payment. Then the next. And the interest is going up and up and she's not being so kind anymore. She says I've abused her trust and her sons aren't happy. She mentions them like this for the first time. All casual.

My sons are not happy, Angelo.

They threaten my wife's mother, my kids are at home and they show up saying they'll do these things if I don't pay. These awful things. They are bad bad people. My wife emails from Malaysia, going crazy with the worry and sometimes weeks go by before I can get back to her and I'm going over and over it thinking… what is happening? I can't sleep. I can't concentrate. Your head makes stories.

Silence.

I am so ashamed that I didn't speak up for you but I had no choice. You have to know that I had no choice.

Pause.

CORRINA. You need to tell someone.

ANGELO. Who? Who can help me?

CORRINA. The union. (*Beat.*) The *Captain*.

ANGELO. Seriously? (*Beat.*) We have a karaoke machine, what do we have to complain about?

Four

The watch. CORRINA *sits on the bridge alone. She stares ahead fighting exhaustion. The 'dead man's alarm' sounds and she jolts awake, jumping up to switch it off.*

She settles back in her chair. Channel 16 crackles a young girl's voice singing along to a clapping game 'My father went to sea sea sea to see what he could see see see but all that he could see see see was the bottom of the deep blue sea sea sea.'

Crackles turn into shouts and laughter then music… the opening lines to 'Corrina, Corrina'.

The voice changes. No accompanying music now just a man's voice singing the third verse of 'Corrina, Corrina' very softly, like a lullaby…

The dead man's alarm blasts out again. CORRINA *jumps to her feet. She presses the alarm off quickly.*

WILL *stands looking at her.*

WILL. I worked with a guy once. One night he's on the bridge and his watch mate starts to feel sick, so rushes off to puke, promises he'll be back in a few minutes. But he's taking ages and the second officer starts to get a bit drowsy. Autopilot's steering though and his mate'll be back soon.

The ship's in the Harima Nada Sea heading toward the Akashi Strait. He knew this route like the back of his hand. Thought he could do it with his eyes shut so he let himself doze a little bit, just seconds at a time. Head keeps jerking up. (*Beat.*) Next thing he's waking up just as the ship's crashing into the sea wall. Two crew died.

Beat.

CORRINA. I wasn't asleep.

WILL. How long have I been stood here then?

CORRINA. I *wasn't* asleep.

WILL. Should report it really, mate.

CORRINA. Report it then. You've been gone half an hour.

WILL. How would you know?

CORRINA. Because I wasn't fucking asleep.

WILL. I *should* report it. But I won't. (*Beat.*) Because I'm not a grass.

Silence. CORRINA *stares straight ahead.*

People's lives in your hands. Need to take your job seriously.

Silence.

WILL *takes his seat.*

Can I ask you something, Corrina?

Silence.

Ten years from now. Where d'you see yourself?

Silence.

Simple question. (*Beat.*) Ten years. Where are you? Ideal world. Where d'you *want* to be? (*Beat.*) Still at sea? (*Beat.*) Or shore based? Don't wanna leave the kids. Fleet manager? What's the plan? Have you got one? (*Beat.*) It's a genuine question. Are you in for the long haul or not? S'all I'm asking.

The radio crackles. Laughter and monkey shrieks.

Because if *this* is what you want to do… what you've really got your heart set on. If you want to move up the ladder… I'd say don't make waves. Terrible fucking pun, mate. Sorry. But you will… you'll get yourself a reputation. (*Beat.*) Have done already. You've probably noticed. (*Beat.*) Made everyone a nervous wreck, mate. All too scared to fuckin' look at yer. Poor Angelo.

Beat.

CORRINA. You threatened him.

WILL. Did he say that?

CORRINA. Didn't have to.

WILL. When you gonna learn? Stop making up stories. Lose all your friends.

CORRINA. You're not my friend.

WILL. Meant Angelo.

CORRINA. Me and Angelo are fine. (*Beat, off* WILL) I wouldn't be so fucking cocky if I were you.

WILL. What's that supposed to mean?

CORRINA. It means he's got a conscience.

Silence. CORRINA *stares ahead.*

WILL. Something like this changes a ship. Build up trust then it's gone, everyone gets back in their box. Captain remembers it too. Sticks in his head. Why would you wanna do that? Remember what you were like at Warsash? You could've got in serious trouble if I wanted to grass you up for anything. But I never would. Wouldn't even cross my mind. 'Cause I know… it's just our thing.

CORRINA. We haven't got a *thing*. We never had a *thing*.

WILL. So you keep saying.

The radio crackles and WILL*'s words play back over it amidst other incoherent jibes.*

Are you jealous?

Beat.

CORRINA. What?

WILL. Of where I am. Being above you. (*Beat.*) You think I don't deserve this? You think it should be you. You're fucked off… is that it? Or is it that I didn't want to make a go of it. With you. Because I did or I sort of did but then we went our different ways and it felt / but anyway that's not the… Is that it? Is that what you wanted?

Beat.

CORRINA. You're delusional.

WILL. Yeah. Right. Cool.

Silence.

CORRINA. I want to do my job. That's all I want to do.

WILL. Fantastic. Me too. So lets do that, hey? Move on. (*Beat.*) No hard feelings.

Silence.

Yeah?

The radio crackles again. Two female voices, coastguards.

Hello ladies.

Silence. A crackle then the voices again.

Both got nice voices. (*Beat.*) I like San Francisco best though, sounds natural. She'd get it. LA's probably fit but I bet she's had loads of work done. Tit job, liposuction. What d'you reckon? Definitely blonde. (*Beat.*) No? Blonde and horny as fuck. Gagging for it.

Silence.

What? You not playing anymore?

Silence.

Fuckin' hell. Bit of banter. Trying to lighten the mood.

Silence.

You've changed. (*Beat.*) You have though. Used to be…

Pause.

CORRINA. What did I used to be?

Beat. WILL *stares at* CORRINA.

WILL. Game.

Five

The CAPTAIN*'s office.* RIZAL *and the* CAPTAIN. *The chessboard laid out.*

CAPTAIN. Before we start… I've got something for you.

From his drawer the CAPTAIN *pulls out a book and hands it to* RIZAL. *It's* Moby Dick.

You might already have it?

RIZAL. No, Sir.

CAPTAIN. Read it far too many times now, I can recite whole bloody chapters by heart. It's a bit battered but I thought you might enjoy it.

RIZAL. Thank you.

CAPTAIN. You're welcome. Let me know what you think.

RIZAL. I will.

RIZAL *puts the book in his bag. The* CAPTAIN *sits down at the chessboard.*

CAPTAIN. Right. Come on. Do your worst, I'm ready for you.

They play.

CAPTAIN. You're religious, Rizal?

RIZAL. I have a strong faith, Sir. Yes.

CAPTAIN. I envy you.

RIZAL. You are not?

CAPTAIN. 'Let faith oust fact, let fancy oust memory; I look deep down and do believe.' (*Beat, nods to the book*) From the book. I think the sea is my heaven, even though I bloody hate it at times.

RIZAL. Well you have *my* God to thank for your heaven.

The CAPTAIN *laughs.*

CAPTAIN. Thanks, Rizal.

RIZAL. …

CAPTAIN. This isn't something I usually do, keep myself to myself, but it's nice to have company sometimes.

RIZAL *nods, a little awkward.*

There's a knock at the door.

Beat.

Come in.

ANGELO *stands in the doorway. A beat as he registers* RIZAL*'s presence, then the chessboard.* RIZAL *looks away.*

ANGELO. Sorry, Sir. I can come back.

CAPTAIN. No no, it's okay. Come on. Come in.

ANGELO *enters. The* CAPTAIN *nods towards the chess board. The atmosphere is suddenly awkward.*

Rizal's teaching me. (*Beat.*) Do you play, Andre?

ANGELO. No, Sir. (*Beat.*) My name is Angelo.

CAPTAIN. Angelo. Sorry. Course it is. What can I do for you, Angelo?

Beat. ANGELO *and* RIZAL *catch eyes briefly.*

ANGELO. I have a problem, Sir. (*Beat.*) With my wages.

CAPTAIN. I'm afraid you'll have to take that up with /

ANGELO. I have spoken to the manning agency. I have called them, I have sent emails. *Lots* of emails. They make promises to look into it and nothing happens.

Silence. ANGELO *looks to* RIZAL. *Beat.* RIZAL *nods, uncomfortable.*

RIZAL. This is true.

ANGELO. I wondered… please, if you could speak to the shipping company? (*Beat.*) On my behalf.

The door opens and WILL *enters, without knocking. He addresses* ANGELO *immediately.*

WILL. The Captain's on a break.

ANGELO. Yes I wanted to /

WILL. Any problems on duty you can come and see me /

CAPTAIN. It's okay, Officer Davis. This is important.

WILL. Sir, whatever this is about /

ANGELO. I have not been paid in four months.

WILL. …

CAPTAIN. Four months? That's outrageous. You should have spoken up sooner.

We'll look into this for you, Angelo. Get it sorted as soon as possible.

ANGELO. Thank you. Thank you, Sir. The situation is / I need money or… it is extremely urgent, Sir.

ANGELO *meets* RIZAL*'s gaze,* RIZAL *looks down.*

WILL *is processing this information – sheer relief.*

CAPTAIN. Officer Davis? Could you help out with this please?

ANGELO *looks to* WILL. *Beat.*

WILL. Of course, Sir. No problem.

ANGELO. Sir, if the *Captain* is involved then surely /

CAPTAIN. You're in good hands with Officer Davis, Angelo. He'll get it sorted for you.

WILL. I will.

Beat. ANGELO *looks to* RIZAL *again.*

Let's go and talk, Angelo.

Beat.

ANGELO. Thank you.

ANGELO *stays where he is.*

WILL. We'll let the Captain finish his break then, yeah?

WILL *gestures to the door. Beat.* RIZAL *watches as* ANGELO *leaves.*

A beat before WILL *follows. The* CAPTAIN *gestures to him.*

CAPTAIN. Thank you, Will.

The door shuts. Beat.

Right, whose move is it?

Six

The karaoke/rec room.

RIZAL *sits reading.* RAFAEL *is watching pornography on a laptop.*

ANGELO *sits away from them at a table.*

CORRINA *enters. She sees the screen and stops.* RAFAEL *stares at her.*

CORRINA *ignores him and takes a seat next to* ANGELO.

RIZAL *shuts* RAFAEL*'s laptop, gesturing to* CORRINA.

RAFAEL. Ano ba! [What are you doing!?]

RAFAEL *puts headphones in and opens the laptop again.*

CORRINA (*to* ANGELO). How you doing?

ANGELO. I made a decision. I'm going home. Soon as we're done with this trip. I'm going back to my family. I go home and I can sort it all out. I can speak to those people, see Angelica face to face. Explain.

CORRINA. What about work?

ANGELO. I'll find work. I don't want this. Not anymore. I want to see my kids. Be a father. I can get another job. People do it. I'll do it. Maybe my wife can come back too. Maybe we'll all go to Malaysia. (*Beat.*) Lots of maybes… lots of possibilities for us.

CORRINA. I hope so.

Beat. ANGELO *takes a small cross from his pocket.*

ANGELO. I know you do not believe but I want to give you this.

CORRINA. What for?

ANGELO. Because I am sorry. Because you were my friend and I let you down.

CORRINA. Angelo it's okay /

ANGELO. Keep it and remember me. Hey, it might protect you from Scylla?

CORRINA. Thanks. (*Pause.*) It's good, Angelo. You should go home. I'm happy for you. I might do the same.

ANGELO. No, man. (*Beat.*) This is your *dream*.

CORRINA. Is it?

ANGELO. Yes! One day when you're Captain, I could come back and work on your ship?

CORRINA. One day I could come and see you in the Philippines. Meet your wife and kids.

Beat.

ANGELO. Maybe, yeah?

CORRINA. What's her name?

ANGELO. My wife? Her name is Amor.

CORRINA. Like love?

ANGELO. Exactly. Like love.

RIZAL *goes to the karaoke machine. He switches it on and sets up the lights.*

He holds out the microphone.

Sinong susunod? [Who's next?]

CORRINA *raises her hand. She stands.*

You are singing? You don't sing.

CORRINA *takes the mic and starts to choose a song. Some muttering from the crew.*

The music starts. And CORRINA *starts to sing 'Jolene' by Dolly Parton.*

ANGELO *watches for a few moments then he stands and leaves.*

CORRINA *doesn't notice him go.*

As CORRINA *sings we watch…*

ANGELO. *On the upper deck. He stands looking out to sea.*

CORRINA *finishes the song.*

Silence in the crew room.

CORRINA *looks around for* ANGELO.

Seven

The ships horn blows. The CAPTAIN *stands before the assembled crew as they observe a minutes silence, heads bowed.*

CAPTAIN. This is a devastating loss.

Pause.

Angelo was a much-respected member of our team. A conscientious, loyal worker… a loving husband and father. (*Beat.*) To say we are all deeply saddened by his passing is a massive understatement.

It feels almost impossible to make sense of a tragedy like this. We can never begin to know what's *really* going on for our colleagues but what we do know is this – we must look out for one another, especially if we sense that others are in need of our help.

We must remember the *human element* of our work.

So… I implore us all to pull together, to keep going for the remainder of our journey… and to honour Angelo's memory as best we can by following his example and working as a team to get the job done.

Silence.

My door is always open.

Eight

The crew room.

A makeshift 'altar' has been erected in honour of ANGELO. *Photographs, candles and various religious ornaments and crosses are arranged on a table which has been pushed against a wall.*

RAFAEL *and* RIZAL *sit before it.* RAFAEL *sings softly. 'Hindi Kita Malilimutan' by Basil Valdez.*

CORRINA *enters. When* RAFAEL *notices her there he stops singing.*

CORRINA *steps forward, she is holding the cross that* ANGELO *gave to her.*

She gestures to the altar.

CORRINA. Can I…?

Beat. RAFAEL *stays silent but he moves to one side to allow* CORRINA *access to the altar.*

CORRINA *places the cross, kneeling down and overcome with emotion.*

RIZAL. Tell me you don't believe in omens now?

Beat.

CORRINA. You think this is my fault?

RIZAL. Not what I said.

RAFAEL. You are not to blame don't worry. Not in that way. I am not superstitious like Rizal. I only believe in what I see.

CORRINA. And what do you see?

RAFAEL. I see people treated like shit, working until the point of exhaustion… I see wages go unpaid for months and months and I see people with power ignoring this because it doesn't affect them.

CORRINA. I haven't got any power, Rafael. Haven't got any power at all.

RAFAEL. More than me.

CORRINA. No. I haven't.

RAFAEL. You are an officer.

Silence.

RAFAEL *gestures to the altar.*

This isn't for you. You are not invited to join us in here. Make your own tribute if you like. Make one with them.

CORRINA. With *them*?

RAFAEL. The officers. Your *people*.

CORRINA. They're not my people.

RAFAEL. Neither are we.

Silence. CORRINA *is crying.*

CORRINA. Angelo was my friend. I wanted him to stand up for himself.

RAFAEL. And there is the problem. (*Beat.*) You think we can stand up for ourselves and win? You think we struggle the same?

CORRINA. Rafael, you know nothing about my struggle /

RAFAEL. You will go home on your nice long shore leave, take it easy, think about your options. What were Angelo's options?

RIZAL. Enough now. It is disrespectful.

RIZAL *gestures to the altar.* RAFAEL *getting increasingly agitated.*

RAFAEL. Who to? Angelo is not here. He's at the bottom of the sea but we're on track for Singapore so hey, everything is okay! No delays and profits are good. 'Keep going and honour his memory.' Phoney bullshit man. Fake fake bullshit these people.

Beat. WILL *and the* CAPTAIN *enter.*

WILL. Your watch started an hour ago.

RAFAEL *gestures to the altar.*

RAFAEL. This is for Angelo Andrada.

CAPTAIN. I understand the need for reflection. This is an extremely… emotional time for everyone.

RAFAEL. Kunwari ka pa. [As if you care.]

WILL. English.

Beat. RAFAEL *is silent*.

CAPTAIN. But the ship cannot come to a standstill.

RAFAEL. Well that is bad luck because we're not working right now.

CAPTAIN. You don't get to decide when work stops.

RAFAEL. A man died.

CAPTAIN. Yes. And you're putting other lives at risk.

RAFAEL. Lives? Or *profits*? What about the *human element*?

CAPTAIN. I look after my crew.

RAFAEL. Do you?

Beat.

RIZAL. Angelo came to you. (*Beat*.) He came and asked for your help because he was in trouble.

CAPTAIN. And I asked Officer Davis to make sure it was dealt with.

WILL. I followed the Captain's orders. But I can't control the outcome. (*Beat*.) Clearly Angelo wasn't in his right mind.

RAFAEL. And why do you think that is?!

WILL. I have no idea /

RAFAEL. Because of this job.

CAPTAIN. You're looking for someone to blame I get that /

RAFAEL. It's your ship. You're the Master.

CAPTAIN. Yes, I am. And I'm giving you an order. Get back to work immediately or you'll be off at the next port.

RIZAL *stands defiant opposite the* CAPTAIN. *He takes the copy of* Moby Dick *from his pocket and throws it at the* CAPTAIN's *feet.*

Beat. The CAPTAIN *leaves.*

WILL. You heard what the Captain said. Get moving.

RAFAEL. Langya ka. [You're shameless.]

WILL. Speak English.

RAFAEL. I said you are shameless.

WILL *steps towards* RAFAEL.

Don't touch me. Don't push me. Keep your hands away.

RIZAL *stands between them. He ushers* RAFAEL *away.*

Beat.

CORRINA. You helped him… you *helped* Angelo?

WILL. Yeah, I did.

CORRINA. I don't believe you.

Beat.

WILL. Believe whatever you want. That's what you do anyway isn't it? (*Beat.*) You're a fantasist, Corrina, your head's fucked.

Beat.

WILL *leaves.*

Nine

Night-time. CORRINA *in her cabin, lying on her bed awake. The dull loud thumping noise followed by the distant sound of music as 'Corrina, Corrina' plays.*

The thumping starts again. She gets up out of bed, trying to trace where it's coming from. It continues, urgent, getting faster.

CORRINA *leaves her cabin, the thumping noise becomes louder, accompanied by snatches of the song, distorted and fleeting.*

CORRINA *searches for the source of the thumping noise which is now gathering pace and becoming almost deafening. She runs to the upper deck, the thumping incessant now, something slamming itself against the boat.*

CORRINA *roars above the noise, a howl of frustration and rage.*

Blackout. In the darkness CORRINA*'s voice comes through on the radio distressed.*

CORRINA (*off-stage*). Will, can you hear me? Are you there?

WILL (*off-stage*). Yes… yeah, yeah I'm here.

CORRINA (*off-stage*). I need help. Please come and help me!

Ten

WILL *is inside the citadel. Radio in hand, obscured by the darkness. The light comes on and* CORRINA *is standing behind him. She locks the door.*

WILL. Are you okay?

CORRINA. Did they see you? Did anybody see you come in?

WILL. No.

CORRINA. Are you sure?

WILL. Yeah.

CORRINA. Lock the door. Lock the fucking door!

WILL *locks the door.*

Give me the keys.

WILL *gives* CORRINA *the keys.*

WILL. What have they done?

CORRINA. Who?

WILL. I don't know. The crew? Corrina, what the fuck's going on?

Beat. CORRINA *starts laughing.*

CORRINA. Your face, mate. (*Beat.*) 'Help me, please help me.' Bouncin' in like fuckin' Bruce Willis on crack.

WILL. I'm confused.

CORRINA. It's a *joke*. (*Beat.*) Here's another one. How many narcissists does it take to change a lightbulb?

Silence.

None. (*Beat.*) They all use gaslighting.

WILL. Okay, great. Let's get back to work.

Silence. CORRINA *stays where she is.*

You're on thin ice as it is. Unlock the door. (*Beat.*) Corrina?

CORRINA. I want to talk.

WILL. ...

CORRINA. Wanna sort things out.

Beat.

WILL. Is that genuine?

CORRINA. Hundred per cent.

WILL. Yeah, well I'd like to put all this… *shit*… behind us.

CORRINA. Me too.

Beat.

WILL. Fuckin'…Good.

Silence.

I am sorry. About Angelo.

CORRINA *nods.*

Not that surprised. You get a sense after a while. Who's got it in them.

CORRINA. I'd say everyone's got it in them.

WILL. Maybe. It's fucking… hard, Corrina. On here. Messes with your head. Everyone defending their corner.

Silence.

Can I be honest?

CORRINA. Yeah.

WILL. I did think something might happen. Between us.

CORRINA. Did you?

WILL. I hoped it might. Yeah.

Silence.

Then you come out with that stuff.

CORRINA. What stuff?

WILL. The shit you said.

CORRINA. About what?

WILL. Come on. About that night.

CORRINA. The night you raped me?

Silence.

WILL. What the fuck is this?

CORRINA. What d'you mean?

WILL. I thought you wanted to move forward.

CORRINA. I am moving forward. This is how I'm going to do it.

WILL. I'm fucking tired, Corrina. I want a quiet life. (*Beat.*) I want this trip to be over and I wanna go home and I wanna go to the pub with me mates. And sleep in me bed. That's what I want. I don't want any more *shit*.

CORRINA. Mate.

WILL. Come on. Let's just fuckin' do this. What do you want?

Beat.

CORRINA. I want you to know a few things. (*Beat.*) I want you to know that you don't get to decide when it stops.

Beat. From behind her back pulls a taser.

WILL. Fuck are you doing?

CORRINA. S'a joke. Lighten up.

WILL. Corrina /

CORRINA. It's not really. Sit on the floor.

WILL *stays standing.*

Sit on the fucking floor.

Silence.

CORRINA *points the taser at him.*

WILL. Alright. Fucking hell.

WILL *crouches down on the floor, leaning against the wall.*

You need to see someone. Big fucking issues you have.

CORRINA. Yes. Yes I have. (*Beat.*) D'you know what my biggest issue is?

Silence.

Having to pretend I'm not frightened. Look at me. (*Beat.*) I'm really good at looking like I'm *not* frightened. I do it every day. All the time. (*Beat.*) From the minute I get up until the minute I go to bed. And even then it doesn't stop because I'm frightened in my sleep. My dad taught me actually. Don't show them you're scared because that makes you *vulnerable. Man up*.

Just fucking *pretend*.

It's alright. I'm okay. I don't mind. It's not a big deal. It's not worth making a fuss.

Pause.

Thing about pretending though is that it gets a bit fucking exhausting after a while. You have to have a lie down. So I lie down and think about it and it's an epiphany; instead of pretending we're not frightened all the fucking time maybe cunts like you could just stop frightening me.

WILL. I never meant to frighten you.

CORRINA. You did more than that.

WILL. I can't even remember.

CORRINA. Can't remember *what?*

Beat.

WILL. That night.

CORRINA. I do. I remember everything. In the bar when it first crossed my mind and thinking it might be something that I wanted. Then in the taxi and you held my hand and I had this feeling like it wasn't right but we were having a laugh and you told me you'd fancied me since basic safety training which feels pretty fucking ironic now. (*Beat.*) Then you sang 'Corrina, Corrina'… the Bob Dylan one and it actually made my stomach turn a bit. Then we were back at yours and I kissed you. I did kiss you. But that was all I wanted. And I remember trying to push you away. (*Beat.*) I was frightened. Really fucking frightened. And I said no. (*Beat.*) Over and over again.

Silence.

WILL. We both had a drink.

CORRINA. So?

WILL. So maybe / I dunno / I might have misread things. (*Beat.*) I'm not making… I'm not making excuses, Corrina.

CORRINA. I think you are.

WILL. I'm sorry.

Silence.

I am sorry… if.

CORRINA. If?

WILL. I am.

CORRINA. Do you know what 'no' means?

Silence.

WILL. I want to sort things out /

CORRINA. Shut the fuck up. (*Beat.*) It's not your turn anymore. It. Is. Not. Your. Turn. Any. Fucking. More.

Silence.

It's *my* turn now.

I'm going to tell you a story. This was my favourite when I was a kid. My dad used to tell it to me.

Once there was a little girl. Princess Scylla. Proper old fashioned one out of a fairy tale. Lived in a castle with her father, the king – very controlling man, told her a load of lies to make sure she never left his side. She had to be a good girl and never betray him.

One day she meets a handsome Prince and she sees a way out. Only he's using her because he wants to become King himself, so after they marry, he kills Scylla's father, then calls her every horrible cunt going, straps her to the front of a ship and sends her off to die a slow miserable death.

Only she doesn't actually die.

She gets stranded. On a desert island. And a sea-witch… whatever the fuck that is, turns her into a monster with six heads. And she's so ashamed of herself that she dives to the bottom of the ocean and stays there.

Meanwhile the new King's having an absolute fucking whale of a time, dripping in gold and jewels, servants at his beck and call. No consequences whatsoever.

He's like a pig in shit.

It never really dawned on me until recently that she got a bit of a rough deal, this princess-monster. There she is. On the seabed. Six heads in twelve hands. Full of shame. Torturing herself. And it's not her fault.

But she can't see that.

In fact it takes her a few thousand years before she can let herself off the hook. Then she gets angry. Then she gets fucking livid. And she swims up to the surface and goes on a rampage, swallowing men on boats like there's no tomorrow.

The sound of thumping begins. WILL *notices, he looks around.*

Used to terrify me when I was a kid, the thought of her, at the bottom of the ocean, watching and waiting for my dad's ship to pass.

Beat. The thumping gets louder and louder.

Now I think… I hope you're getting enough to eat, love.

CORRINA *raises the taser towards* WILL, *pointing it directly at him.* WILL *cowers, holding his hands over his head.*

A loud THUMP and then blackout.

Eleven

ANGELO *stands on the upper deck looking out to sea. He sings 'Corrina, Corrina'.*

CORRINA *appears on the deck below. She walks slowly to the front of the ship, taking over from* ANGELO *as she begins to sing the chorus.*

Blackout.

The End.

A Nick Hern Book

Corrina, Corrina first published in Great Britain as a paperback original in 2022 by Nick Hern Books Limited, The Glasshouse, 49a Goldhawk Road, London W12 8QP, in association with Headlong and Liverpool Everyman & Playhouse

Cover image: Feast Creative

Designed and typeset by Nick Hern Books, London
Printed in Great Britain by Mimeo Ltd, Huntingdon, Cambridgeshire PE29 6XX

A CIP catalogue record for this book is available from the British Library

ISBN 978 1 83904 104 4